Edward Jenkins

Lord Bantam

Edward Jenkins

Lord Bantam

ISBN/EAN: 9783743337145

Manufactured in Europe, USA, Canada, Australia, Japa

Cover: Foto ©ninafisch / pixelio.de

Manufactured and distributed by brebook publishing software (www.brebook.com)

Edward Jenkins

Lord Bantam

BY
EDWARD JENKINS
AUTHOR OF "GINX'S BABY."

FIFTH EDITION

STRAHAN & CO.
56, LUDGATE HILL, LONDON
1872

LONDON:
PRINTED BY VIRTUE AND CO.
CITY ROAD.

CONTENTS.

PART I.

HOW HE CAME INTO THE WORLD.

		PAGE
I.	Delicate Announcements	1
II.	Preliminaries	4
III.	A Land Slip	10
IV.	A Son	16
V.	The First Accident	18

PART II.

HOW HE CAME TO BE LORD BANTAM.

I.	A Human Feeding Bottle	20
II.	Passages from a Diary	24
III.	Academic Groves	32
IV.	A young Aristocrat	34

PART III.

HOW HE LEARNED HIS LETTERS.

I.	Words versus Wit	39
II.	Digression. Benevolently dedicated to American Readers	41

		PAGE
III.	A Juvenile Tourist and Author	43
IV.	A Scotch Tutor	47
V.	Catholicism	59
VI.	Agape	67
VII.	Human Sympathy in its Influence on Catholicity	70
VIII.	Oxbridge	73
IX.	The Radish Club	75
X.	The Essenes	77

PART IV.

HOW HE CAME TO YEARS OF DISCRETION AND OTHERWISE.

I.	Citizen Bantam	82
II.	A Rank Communist	85
III.	A School for Fledgling Nobles	89
IV.	A Proletarian Compliment	93
V.	Newspaper Moralizers	103
VI.	Economic Notes	105
VII.	Land and Economy	112
VIII.	A Startling Lecture	116

PART V.

HOW HE BECAME A LEGISLATOR.

I.	A Vacancy	123
II.	Diversities of Operations	127
III.	Taking no Part in it	131
IV.	Fencing	137
V.	Party Tactics	139
VI.	Marching Orders	143
VII.	Too Much of a Good Thing	146
VIII.	An Election Manœuvre	149

		PAGE
IX.	A Fogy Candidate	155
X.	Electoral Skirmishing	157
XI.	Canvassing Extraordinary	160
XII.	Inconvenient Results of Popular Reform	165
XIII.	Explosion—of a totally new Fulminating Agent	168
XIV.	The Press express their Opinions	172
XV.	M.P.	174
XVI.	Disaster to a Prig Ministry	175
XVII.	The Claims of Society on its Gods	179
XVIII.	Nobility and the Working Man	182

PART VI.

HOW HE EMBRACED THE ECLECTIC RELIGION.

I.	Society—at large	187
II.	Developing the Mental and Moral Stamina of Woman	193
III.	The Eclectic Religion	202
IV.	Eclecticism in Raptures	207
V.	By Civil Contract	212
VI.	An Eclectic Symposium	216

PART VII.

HOW HE COQUETTED WITH THE PROLETARIAT.

I.	Practical Antidotes of Philosophic Theories	222
II.	The Creed of Party	224
III.	Parliamentary Consciences	229
IV.	Priest Politics	230
V.	Transmontane Secrets	233
VI.	A Willing Sacrifice	235
VII.	Transmontane Reformers	236
VIII.	A New Charter	237

	PAGE
IX. Death and Sunshine	240
X. Party *versus* Principles	244
XI. A Constitutional Crisis	246

PART VIII.

HOW HE CAME TO HIS ESTATE.

I. The Ruling Passion strong in Death	254
II. In the Grain	257
III. Philosophy and Fact	259

PART I.

HOW HE CAME INTO THE WORLD.

I.—Delicate Announcements.

ON the fifth day of April, A.D. 18— the following announcement appeared in the PICCADILLY JOURNAL:—

SONS.

FFOWLSMERE, Countess of, on the 1st .inst., at 20, Hiton Place.

The excitement created by the event thus drily and statistically chronicled was not confined to the distinguished lady and the little individual of the species under which he was classified. In Lord Ffowlsmere's noble breast, in that general bosom which every Englishman's family is said to possess, and in the society wherein the Earl and Countess of Ffowlsmere were distinguished political leaders, the birth thus baldly scheduled sent a thrill of unusual feeling.

There is nothing wonderful in the birth of a son, even among the higher aristocracy when married; why, then, may some inquisitive person ask, should there be any rare excitement when to Lady Ffowlsmere happened so commonplace an accident? So might I, along with several million compatriots of the Ffowlsmere family have inquired, who were not sufficiently high-bred to know the causes that agitate the inner circles of society: and, as a fact, we should have been as ignorant of the trepidation as of its reason, had not the *Piccadilly Journal* printed a few days after the advertisement the following paragraph :—

"We understand that the Countess of Ffowlsmere is progressing very favourably since the birth of a son on the 1st instant. It is a curious fact that her ladyship's last child, the present Lord Bantam, and heir to the peerage, was born so far back as June 18—, a period of nearly nineteen years."

This delicate intimation awakened in my mind an interest in the fate of the boy who seemed to have been born out of time, and from that day to this I have closely followed the changes of his history. My original curiosity was to ascertain how Earl Ffowlsmere would deal with the editor of the *Piccadilly Journal* or of the medical review from which the information had been clipped, but he appeared to have been too indifferent or too haughty to horsewhip those egregious prigs. The information, however, having come to me through this public channel, I am entitled to use it. The disclosure in question amply accounts for much emotion on the part of the Earl and Countess of Ffowlsmere, and a very pretty gossip throughout the vast bounds of their acquaintanceship.

I have rather reflected on the *Piccadilly Journal*, but I will report a conversation, overheard about the same time at the Hon. Mrs. Trippety's ball. The personages were none other than Lady Eaton, Mrs. Everard Chesham, and those charming girls the two Misses Du Pont.

MRS. CHESHAM. Have you heard the news? O, so funny! Lady Ffowlsmere has a son.

LAURA DU PONT. O, nonsense, *dear* Mrs. Chesham. You must be mistaken. Why, Lord Bantam is over eighteen, and there are no other children. It's quite impossible.

MRS. CHESHAM. Hush, dear, you don't know what's possible or impossible. I'm sure it's true, because our carriage drove over the straw as we came here to-night.

LADY MARY EATON (convinced by this evidence). I'm afraid it is true; but really, is it not most extraordinary! If I were Lady Ffowlsmere, I could never show my face in London again. Why, it's really shocking! It's like a loosis—loosis—

MRS. CHESHAM. *Naturæ*, dear; you oughtn't to try Latin words, you know. But, indeed, that expresses exactly what it ought to be called—poor thing!

Et cetera, et cetera, et cetera.

If the female part of society was scandalized by the frank announcement in the *Piccadilly Journal*, the Editor, for his part, might have retorted on the ladies, that his knowledge of society afforded him ground to believe himself, as regarded that, quite *en rapport* with them.

II.—Preliminaries.

How Lady Ffowlsmere's baby came into the world is a matter involving, on my part, such sacred and even translunary knowledge, that I almost fear, if I proceed to divulge the facts, I shall either lose credit with every one for truthfulness, or be suspected of some Satanic means of information.

The common bantling of Mrs. Ginx may come into the world with somewhat rough concomitancy of circumstances, but what are the happy accidentia of a birth like that of Lady Ffowlsmere's baby?

As to Lady Ffowlsmere herself, she was the subject of several months' astonishment. She looked at young Lord Bantam when he came home from Winton with sensations of awkward wonder. How long ago it seemed since he was little baby Bantam, laughing and coughing in her young ladyship's lap. Now, after a pause of nineteen years, after she had buried the hopes of rejuvenescent motherhood, when she had thrown herself with rare ability and *finesse* into political intrigue, and had become the social head of the feminine Prig clique—now, when she was almost regarded as a states*man*, or,

PRELIMINARIES.

at all events, as a most noble, most charming, but confirmed political *intriguante*, here, by a ridiculous accident, she was obliged to await an event which she knew would make her the laughing-stock of society. I am bound to believe that she never spent so uncomfortable a period in her life.

None the less needful was it to prepare for the coming trouble in true aristocratic fashion.

Every morning at eleven, for six months, Sir Samuel Hornbill, F.R.C.S., whose distinguished services to royalty in difficulties had procured him honours rarely to be won in any other medical or surgical field, visited her ladyship and chatted with her for ten minutes, while she, enveloped in a rich Cashmere robe, took chocolate out of an elegant Dresden service, presented by as pretty a little maid as ever distressed a footman's heart. Later in the day, her ladyship took an airing. Gillow, the coachman, was instructed to drive with double caution, and above all to avoid taking her ladyship in the direction of any street row, monster, or accident. It was the groom's special duty to keep on the watch for extraordinary instances of deformity or ugliness on either side of the way, and to warn the maid, who forthwith diverted her ladyship's attention until they were past the dangerous object. One thing of which the Countess had a rooted dislike was red hair. The most disagreeable relation of her husband's family was a red-headed Marquis, and him she hated so cordially that his hair could scarcely escape her resentment. Blinks, therefore—whose own locks were snow-white with floury filth—was strictly cautioned not to permit a carrot-head, aristocratic or plebeian, to come within the range of his mistress's vision. Poor Blinks! He was sitting on the box one day, at the Corner, when that pretty Jemima Mosely, the under-nurse at Lord Evergood's, was passing with the little lords and ladies out for an airing, and never saw the fiery locks of the Marquis of Arran, who, recognising the carriage, actually rode up to the wheel, and, uncovering his orange-tawny pate, bowed it portentously forward almost in the Countess's lap. Lady Ffowlsmere, giving a little shriek, buried her face in her handkerchief. The Marquis thought she had gone mad, and went off blazing like a turkey cock. Blinks, after handing the Countess up the steps at Hiton Place, packed his clothes and left without waiting for his wages or any formal excommunication. He felt like a man who had committed murder.

The children of rank and wealth are taken care of before they are born. What are we to expect of the babes whose mothers carry them where awful, devil-features abound, and where grotesqueries of Hell are the environments of their daily life?

For months before the arrival of Lady Ffowlsmere's baby, her ladyship was dangerously excited about his *natalia*. Almost daily the carriage went to Williams's, whose shop windows are a perfect and open instruction to any observant bachelor in all the mysteries of feminine or infantile equipment.

—Ah! well I remember how one day sauntering in Regent Street I saw my lovely little cousin Angela in her pretty brougham drive up to such a shop, with its white-lined windows there before me, and that mysterious word LAYETTES in gilded characters upon the cornice, and I, awkward idiot that I was, stood talking, and never saw the changing pinks upon the sweet young face, and even begged she would let me be her groom for the nonce, and hand her to the counter; and she, how perplexed she was, and how shy, and she said she thought she would not stay there just now, she had just driven to the pavement to see *me*—the little storyteller!—and how I, a few days after, lounging over the *Chimes* at the club, saw the announcement of her first infant, and, as I recalled the scene, the shop, the embarrassment, my great coarse face and ears grew red and hot with shame, that I should have been so thick a fool! I reverenced her ever after for that true, godly touch of shy innocence, and everywhere I see it I recognise it as a pure relic of Eden.—

But I come back to Williams's. In the midst of white and coloured *robes de jour et de nuit*, was a bust of a Royal Princess, fitted with an exquisitely-shaped corset of blue satin edged with ermine. Other nameless shadows of form, elaborately fine, were arranged in suggestive positions. Why in ordinary life it should be considered right to conceal such pretty mysteries beneath conventional robes, yet proper to expose them to every rude gaze in this manner, has long been to me a matter of speculation. It is useless to say that the stronger half of creation should shut its eyes to what is put under its noses. Is there any necessity for the exposure? Our old English prudery—now alas! fast dying out, and it was a grand, dignified, purific sentiment—used to be based on this: to avoid by look or gesture, by hint or display, anything however distantly exciting the imagination in a wrong direction. It was a point of training with our mothers and grandmothers and the society they adorned.

"*Mais! nous avons changé tout cela!*" cries Mrs. Croquet, and we all admit she is a charming woman. "We are no longer afraid to call a spade a spade; and I am happy to say my daughters are strong-minded enough to read, or see, or say anything without the slightest sense of impropriety. Laura made a speech the other day for the hospital for lying-in women, and went into the whole question of the reasons for their being there; and every one was astounded at her freedom from the silly restraints of conventional decorum. Evil be to him that evil thinks. To the pure, all things are pure. What a man can do, a woman may. I have no notion of your mawkish decency. It often serves for a mere cover to impurity."

Dear Madam! I wish your apophthegms were relevant and true; I wish your theories were consistent with the facts of human nature! I have seen rare girls demoralised, nay lost by association with foul ideas; and God forbid my little daughter, whose tender freshness is the most piquant joy of my life, whose jealously-guarded simplicity is my daily burden and hope, should ever come to know more than she does of the unnameable, or, as a matter of moral pride, unsex herself to win what I can only call a foul and tawdry admiration.

This though is a sheer digression from Lady Ffowlsmere's preparations. They were extensive enough to have stocked a bazaar. Robes miraculously embroidered, mantlets trimmed with ermine, long gowns and short coats, night dresses and day frocks, flannels decorated with herring-bone stitch, diminutive—but there, I need not schedule everything. The coming little Bantam, male or female, had a wardrobe of clothes before it drew breath. In the North of Ireland a christening-robe was being embroidered to cost a hundred guineas.

The bassinet was a picture. Messrs. Jackson and Graham lavished upon its production all their classic skill. It was a white and gold shell, swung by gilded cords from two Italian pillars, and was, they slily informed her ladyship, in the purest *Renaissance* style. Delicate sky-silk hangings, subdued by the finest muslin, drooped round the shell; and the Countess used to go and hang over it, and wonder what little form would press the downy bed and satin-like pillow.

III.—A Land Slip.

The Earl of Ffowlsmere was one of the wealthiest men in the three kingdoms. His possessions in agricultural counties, in mineral districts, in the metropolis —not to mention half the vast manufacturing town of Ironchester—were so enormous and their returns so lucrative, that the public may be forgiven for attributing to him fabulous riches, and entertaining itself with calculations that every second of the day or night the Earl was receiving a sum equivalent to a respectable man's salary for a year.

A clever ancestor of the Earl, duly encouraged and assisted by the laws of these realms, happening, by good luck to him, to possess land that grew in great request for the houses of a pushing population, had been able to grant leases of it to various tenants for just ninety-nine years. In effect, this was to keep the real ownership of the land in abeyance while two or perhaps three generations lived and died, and then, long after the clever old man was in his grave, to cause the immensely enhanced freehold to fall in to a person he had never seen, and whom he could only prophetically and vaguely designate as the next heir of some one. It was the merest " fluke "—if I may use a felicitous vulgarism—that the Earl of Ffowlsmere's father happened to be that fortunate next heir. He had done or conceived of nothing on earth to entitle him to take a vast property, a noble name, a place in the legislature of the country, the right of nominating a hundred clergy to as many perishing flocks: all that fell upon him simply by fate and the custom of England. In defiance of economy, a vast piece of land was locked up for those ninety-nine years from public enterprise and general exchange. No one could build on it anything but what was permitted by the terms of the leases. One term, for instance, had been that no shops were to be opened upon the land. No shops were or could be opened, and the line of healthy trade was blocked out of a large area to be sent winding about in neighbouring slums and byways. No churches other than those of the Establishment were to be erected within the sacred precincts. Hence every dissenter who lived there was forced to worship, like a leper in Israel, "without the camp." The natural and legitimate changes which pass over such areas in great cities—the transformation of dwellings into places of business, or of moderate houses into palaces, in fact, every concomitant of natural progress was baulked in this district by the ninety-nine year leaseholds working with the laws and customs of this realm. Progress had to pass over and round it, and at great inconvenience to find expansion further off. It is scarcely possible to trace out with fulness the vicious effects of the laws under which such a prescription was legal. How it locked up for years from public competition, from healthy and beneficent activity of exchange, hundreds upon hundreds of properties; how it restrained —as we have seen—the uses to which the properties might have been put; how it limited the number of persons in the community that could possibly gain livelihood or profit from the existence of the land; how it affected the character and architecture of the buildings erected on the soil; how, in fact, the tendency of this arrangement was to diminish in a certain proportion for every man in England the chances—chances that have an important influence upon the enterprise and vigour of the greater number of people in a state—of acquiring landed property. In fact, it is no untruth to say that the State had permitted this old peer, in common with half a hundred more, to rob posterity of possibilities of action and advantage to which it was righteously entitled.

I have said it was by the merest *fluke* that the present Lord Ffowlsmere's father happened to be the person described as the next heir. But it is some compensation to know that he was the very person whom the venerable grantor of leases, had he been alive, would have given his eyes not to see in possession. It happened in this wise.

Earl Ffowlsmere, fifth Earl, had issue by Caroline his wife a son and a daughter. Son married the Hon. Lucinda Lucretia Bella De Lancey, daughter of Nugent-Nugent, Earl of Foswick, by whom he had issue three sons—I need not name them, for they all died unmarried, and there was an eno of that line. While they were living and dying, the reversions of all the leases made by the fifth Earl, were hovering about in the clouds waiting to descend and light down on a certain day in a certain year upon any one who was so fortunate as to be properly in the way.

The only daughter of Caroline, Countess of Ffowlsmere, made a sad mistake, for she fell in love with the gayest and handsomest man in the army, Captain Harrow of the —th Hussars, ran away with him and married him at Gretna Green. Whereupon the Earl cursed her and hers, and forbad her his presence for evermore. Should he perchance have reached heaven his aristocratic wish may deprive poor Honoria of the joys of Paradise; should he have gone elsewhere she may not altogether regret the proscription. Captain Harrow found that he could not keep both his family and his regiment, so he sold out. Every year Honoria presented him with a diminutive fresh Harrow, and this drove him to try his fortunes in trade—the wine trade. A dragoon in the wine trade is a fish in the water, but certainly not in his proper element; and poor Captain Harrow, tasting too freely of his wares, lost by degrees his fine gentleman's manner, his clear manly voice, his moulded features, his gallant honour—and fell: no matter where. Honoria would never own the change in her heart's man, and shut from her vision the sickly sense of it that often came over her. She would love him all the same: and when at last hard want enjoined it; she worked from yellow morn to dusky eve, away up in a sky pent-house, toiled and kept a dying man with the craving children for months and months, with the energy of those white, blue-coralled fingers, till even the hag who owned the house and exacted the rent grew sorry and sympathetic. So on, so on, till one day Harrow died. Then Honoria broke down, and lay there stony-hearted, stony-looking, by the body—lay while the children wondered that papa and mamma did not move or talk. The woman sent away to a well-known association to say that a man had died and a woman was dying in her house. By some God's chance there came a General, interested in the society, who volunteered to investigate the case. When he took the face-cloth from the dead man's face he recognised an early friend. Within a few hours Honoria opened her eyes on a comfortable room, pervaded with warmth such as she had not felt about her for many a day, a soft bed and her children transformed, smiling at the transformation. A few hundred pounds collected from former friends of her husband,—the old Earl would do nothing,—placed her in a country town where there was a free school. There she decently brought up her children and there she died. Her eldest boy married a pretty damsel, daughter of a not over rich vicar, and following his father's example surrounded himself with little shoots. His son and heir became a schoolmaster, who taking a fancy to a decent housekeeper at a neighbouring park, also married and maintained the Bantam line. Imagine the surprise of this worthy couple, always proud of the tradition of their descent, but hopeful of no good from it, when one day a breathless attorney rushes by train into the town, with rapid and distracted inquiries finds them out, and informs them, listening aghast, that Master Eugene George Augustus Harrow, aged ten, is heir to unlimited estates, and will be the richest man in the three kingdoms! For the ninety-nine year leases were shortly to fall in, and the reversion was to descend upon the very last person whom the fifth Earl would have wished to benefit. The present Earl had been that lucky boy. Reared in a school of adversity—a man of iron rigidity of character—he was celebrated for his thrift in the management of his almost regal estate. His business talents enabled him to develop its productive capabilities, spite of the legal parasites that everywhere and always sought to feed upon the plethoric body. He was an attorney and a tradesman in a peer's robes. Proud of his riches, his pride led him to take care that they should not be carelessly distributed. He watched every penny of expenditure, every item of income. The aforesaid parasites were checked though not always thwarted—they were too clever for that—at every turn.

The Earl had one grotesque peculiarity. In his youth, he had heard his father sing with much spirit, a comic song entitled "The Cork Leg." Some of the stanzas adhered to his memory and suggested a strange community between himself and the hero of them. When alone and unoccupied with business he invariably repeated them to himself:—

> In Holland there dwelt a Mynheer Von Clam,
> Who every morning said, 'I am
> The richest merchant in Rotterdam.'

IV.—A Son.

THE day at length arrived when the Countess must face the cross of woman's curse. No avoidance—no circuity—it stood in her life-path, and she should either pass it or die at its base. Herein my lady and Mrs. Ginx are one.

Through the vast regions of the mansion thrilled subdued excitement. Some of its tenants were anxious—some foolish. There was the grave butler, the discountenanced footman, the deeply-agitated cook, the shocked or giggling maids; and all stepped lightly over the velvet carpets gossiping only in whispers. The Earl retired to his library, where he pretended to himself to be reading a blue-book report on the condition of his own tenantry in various shires. In her ladyship's room——no matter: there were Sir Samuel Hornbill, Mr. Burton, F.R.C.S., and the nurse; who require neither you nor me with any impertinent curiosity.

    *   *   *   *   *   *   *   *

Happily the Countess passed through the gate of sorrow, faced and went by the painful cross—and a piping little voice in the next room seemed to her, lying in a half-senseless dream, to come and go like a soft, glad music.

"A son, Countess," whispered Sir Samuel, mildly. "I congratulate you."

A palpitating maid outside the chamber had run to the footman at the head of the stairs, and the footman had carried his mighty legs swiftly down to the butler who waited in the hall; and the butler, almost void of speech, had precipitated himself through the library-door and caught the Earl with the agricultural blue-book in his hand, standing at the mantel-piece, blanched with anxiety, which he endeavoured to repress by repeating to himself:—

> In Holland there dwelt a Mynheer Von Clam,
> Who every morning said, 'I am
> The richest merchant in Rotter—

When in burst Trayfoot the butler—

—DAM'

said the Earl, in his nervousness, involuntarily repeating that syllable out very loud as he turned round.

"I 'umbly beg pardon, your lawdship," gasped Trayfoot, clearly spelling the syllable the wrong way, and dumbfounded by the Earl's vehemence, "but if you please my lawd it's a son and her Ladyship's as well as could be expected."

⁎

V.—The First Accident.

"THANK God," said the Earl, and leaving the bewildered Trayfoot to reconcile this expression with the other, set to work reading at his blue-book in the sheer excitement of pleasure.

The eminent surgeon and his coadjutor had gone: the Countess was to receive a visit from the Earl before she was settled for the night. Softly he entered the room, slipped over the moss-like carpet, and stood beside the purple hangings of the bed. Gently he caressed a moment the pale, sweet, glorified face,—glorified by the joy that had come out of pain.

COUNTESS. Have you seen him?

EARL. No.

COUNTESS. Neither have I.

EARL (whispering to the nurse, whose back appeared through the door). Struthers, bring the baby.

She brought him in. The Earl fetched a candle, the nurse held up the little lace-swathed honourable, the Countess turned languidly towards her child—no sooner turned than she uttered a shriek and fainted away. The Earl dropped the candle—the nurse dropped the baby.

—The little honourable's head was the colour of a Maltese orange.

PART II.

HOW HE CAME TO BE LORD BANTAM.

I.—A Human Feeding Bottle.

HAD the young honourable fallen on his head his yellow hair had been the death of him. He luckily touched the ground elsewhere,—in fact with a part not vital. Beyond a little screaming, he showed no sign of harm. He was otherwise quite a pretty baby, and the obnoxious hair being concealed for a few weeks under a cap, her Ladyship grew accustomed to him, though she vowed eternal enmity to her cousin of Arran.

I believe no Countess ever thinks of nursing her own baby. Middle and low class people enjoy a monopoly of that privilege. I think if I were a woman—and it is the best thing I could wish to be this side of heaven —I could imagine no greater ecstasy than to enfold with motherly arms my own flesh and blood, while it drew from me, a consciously pure fountain, the spring-flow of life. But to some minds that would seem to be too vulgar a sympathy. At all events, the Countess required a proper young woman not embarrassed with matrimonial trammels yet in a situation to perform a mother's part; such an one as is frequently described by the advertisement, "As wet nurse. Fine breast of milk. Single; highly respectable."

Mr. Burton was consulted.

" Burton, mind you get a proper person. *Please* be careful. You don't know how terribly I should feel it if the woman were not perfectly healthy. Inquire into her antecedents. See the other members of her family and ascertain if they have any deformity or peculiarity, especially insanity. Young Airsleigh's singularity, you know, is directly traceable to his nurse's aunt, who was a low sort of Radical—a preacher in some odd dissenting sect. And, by the way, that reminds me,—inquire if she has been baptized and confirmed and properly churched—for though we are Populars you know we must not go too far—and don't get a shocking creature with red hair, whatever you do!"

Mr. Burton, like most members of his profession, managed to satisfy his patient's whims without paying the least heed to them. He went to his own hospital, where a sort of wet-nurses' fair was held every morning, and picking out a fresh-looking young woman, who declared herself unembarrassed and held a visibly healthy baby in her arms, informed her that she and her progenitors had never been dissenters, had always been of exceedingly sound mind and body, that she herself was an accredited member of the Church of England, and must forthwith go and be churched. A well-known author has touchingly told how, by the rigorous rule of the society in which the Countess moved, the poor women who are hired to supply strength to infant Bantams are bound over to desert their own children absolutely, to have no interviews with any relatives during the time of their engagement, and to do their best to keep themselves in good health.

I think, my lady, you would have been touched had you seen her, when the hard bargain was concluded, clinging to the baby as one would do who was never to see it again. . . . . Indeed the child of fortune was destined to rob the child of fate. The nurse's fine little girl was consigned to a neighbour, whose trade it was to "farm" such deserted ones, and sadly did a mother's forebodings about the dubious kindness of the baby-farmer pierce her heart as she gave up the child. True and fearful instinct! When she kissed the small face, and wrapped the little form as tenderly as possible in her coarse shawl, she might as well have buried it alive then and there. It was the last kiss, the last look for her—the last touch of joy for that little one on earth. Eight months after, when young Bantam took to pap and his nurse came out of the palatial tomb, the cab she hired in her maternal eagerness took her—Heaven help me! I cannot tell you the rest. Imagine it, if you please, for yourself. The woman's sin had been buried out of her sight.

Rackett's place, Rackett was the woman's name, in the mansion at Hiton Place, was, to tell the truth, simply to be a human feeding-bottle. Her foster-child was not confided to her care. She was not even permitted to enjoy the thousand pleasures to a true natural woman, of tending and caressing the infant she suckled. When the young Bantam grew hungry, and signified it by vulgar screams, he was conveyed by the extremely lady-like person who was called his nurse to Rackett's room, and she when his cravings were satisfied delivered him up again. Very strict orders had been given by her Ladyship that the person was not to kiss the child on any pretence, but I fear all concerned were too womanly to obey her orders.

I have gone into these nursery details, your Royal Highnesses, my Lords, Ladies and Gentlemen, not because I like to discuss such matters, but because they are true and common as life, and yet mayhap will wear a strangely novel aspect when thus put down in black and white. I should be sorry to think so meanly of your sensibilities as to suppose that the sketch will simply amuse you.

* *
*

II.—Passages from a Diary.

THE young honourable took kindly to Rackett's attentions, and his body and the golden hair grew together. I cannot afford to waste much space over his infantile experiences. He fed, he hiccoughed, he drivelled, he screamed, he kicked, like any other baby: he passed through every phase of catarrh: but then he was bathed in porcelain, swathed in lawns and laces, embroideries and velvet; he lay in the Renaissance cradle with the soft-hued curtains drawn around him keeping out the evil-tempered air. He was watched and waited on by half-a-dozen servants, guarded in his airings by a careful groom, handled and dandled like a humming-bird's egg. So valuable a contribution to the population of these kingdoms must be reared, spite of accident or fate. Messrs. Malthus and Mill never put their heads inside a nobleman's house to forbid the banns or play the part of cross-legged Juno. Yet it would require many philosophic treatises to prove to me that my young Bantam, as he lay and fluttered in the Renaissance shell, was any more likely than the child of some sturdy navigator rolling in a washerwoman's basket to be in the long run useful to society. Might he not become a *roué*, a rake, a screw, a Fogy, or even a Prig?

Lady Ffowlsmere kept a diary. It was a wonderful conglomeration. Among other things were occasional hints of her baby's life. The Countess's royal mistress had set a fashion for keeping such records. In volumes guarded by handsome Chubb's locks, she had very simply and prettily written down from time to time her home experiences, and every Court lady for awhile took to a similar historiography, not always I fear so pure and true as hers—much to Mr. Chubb's advantage. Magnificent bindings, illuminated monograms, and marvellous mechanisms with gold keys often enclosed from profane vision some of the least or some of the most extraordinary things in the world. The Countess wrote a swift running hand. I find, in looking through the volume, among social and political gossip, a few scandals, notes of sermons preached at St. Elias's Chapel, Ely Square, others of new fashions, a tolerably constant account at first of little Master Bantam's doings, whence I extract the following memorabilia:—

"*May* 10. Baby christened by the Bishop of Dunshire. Cousin Duke of Scrambleton and dear Lady Goding Goding were the godfather and godmother. Ffowlsmere and I had a great deal of difficulty in selecting his names, our circle is so large. It was impossible to please everybody. He was christened Albert Alfred Augustus Adolphus Loftus Ciceley Chester: we mean to call him Albert. We had a very pleasant party afterwards. What a charming man the bishop is! So brilliant, so well-bred, so perfectly a man of the world, yet so pious, so sympathetic and sentimental, with such soft and delicate hands. He is a thorough Churchman, and an exquisite gentleman. I often wonder why people ridicule him so much. He is so able. He goes about so mildly, and seems to have no evil whatever in him. When I see him, I cannot help thinking 'of such is the kingdom of heaven'—though I don't think he is a 'little child' *quite*."

Here is rather an irrelevant but interesting entry:

"*June* 2. Cabinet Council to-day. Ffowlsmere says the ministers are very uneasy about the attitude of the Extremists in the House. Some of them are very fractious, and there is ground to believe that they have been angling with the other side for a coalition. That must be impossible, though in the present state of parties one knows not what to expect. Ffowlsmere thinks they want office, but it is out of the question to take any of them into the Cabinet, as he and the other Prigs would instantly retire. They belong to a new and dangerous school of politics; in fact, it is said some of them are Communists. They charge the Government with too much political intrigue and too little real reform; and indeed I think they are not so far wrong in that. I never saw it so difficult to keep a Government together. It takes all my wit to manage these new vulgarians. Besides there are two or three men in the Cabinet who are enough to swamp any ministry. Tandem is always going to do something, and never does it. Some one in the House said **the** other night, that he wished the President of the Board would be true to his name, and *at length* do something. Happily many of these Extremists are more loud than dangerous. They don't like to risk their chance of office, though they are obliged every now and then to express violent opinions. I found out last evening that Mingo's wife and daughter are dying **to** be presented, and must manage it for them. Tumbril is troublesome. He **has** a large family, and I must show them some attention. Ay me! Politics is a troublesome affair."

Further on I find that Mingo's wife and daughter have been duly presented, and that he was behaving much more reasonably, but that Tandem still, to the distraction of his colleagues, **pursued his** wavering and unproductive career.

"*June* 23. Little **Albert was** this morning seized with twitchings in the face soon after feeding; his mouth worked fearfully, and there seemed to be a discharge from it. I sent at once for Mr. Burton, **who came in** haste and pronounced it to be nothing but *colic*. I at once sent for Mrs. Rackett and blew her **up.** . . . .

"*Sept.* 5. (Shufflestraw Castle). **We** had a great alarm to-day with little Albert. I went into the nursery, and found him screaming with might and main. His face was *scarlet*. Swanston could not pacify him; and though he was taken to Mrs. Rackett, he would not be quiet. At length it seemed *certain* it would end in *convulsions*; and Mr. Bellew was fetched from Rotherhedge. He was unpleasantly calm about it, and said no boy could be very ill who screamed like that. He insisted on taking off his clothes, and found that Swanston's maid, in dressing the poor little fellow, had bound a *nursery pin* tightly into his little back, so as to mark him severely! It was so grossly careless, I instantly dismissed her. I am glad to see that his hair is getting a little browner.

"*Sept.* 20. We are full of company—a great shooting party with us. The bishop is here, and stays at home with the ladies. I haven't much time for little Albert. Mr. Bellew vaccinated him to-day, from a very fine child, after a careful examination to decide whether he was strong enough to bear it.

"*Sept.* 24. Albert's vaccination took: he is very feverish and restless. I asked Mr. Bellew, and he tells me he never knew it to be fatal.

"*Sept.* 25. Albert's arm very much inflamed. Swanston says he is a screamer, and attributes it to his red hair. She says all children with red hair are bad tempered. What a *pity*, to be sure! Otherwise he is perfect.

"I've had a most terrible fright. The person Mr. Bellew brought to the castle the other day, with her child, to vaccinate Albert from, was recognised by some of the servants, and *it turns out that she is the wife of that shoemaker Broadbent, who is an infidel Chartist!!!*

the plague of the town. He is repeatedly addressing meetings and getting up opposition to us at elections, and has insulted the vicar by calling him 'an ecclesiastical speaking-trumpet.' I was most *indignant* that such *shocking* blood should be transferred to poor little Albert, and sent for Mr. Bellew immediately. He had nothing to say for himself, except that it was the healthiest child in the neighbourhood! I told him he ought to have known that though we were free in our politics, we hated such vulgar and seditious wretches; and it was an everlasting disgrace to us to have their brand on a scion of our house. The Earl gave him a cheque, and he is never to enter the castle again. I have sent to town for Mr. Burton to come and see him. I shall be in terror now, lest the child has been inoculated with some low *Red* opinions. The Earl says he is not likely, with the property he will get, to practise them, even if they are in his blood; but I have the utmost horror of extremists."

The Countess was unquestionably a Prig.

Later on I find little scraps here and there which I need not date. "Albert beginning to teeth. Mr. Burton has been to see him every day for a fortnight. Albert terribly cross." The family have evidently returned to town and Mr. Burton again. "Steedman's soothing-powder to Albert." "Gave Albert magnesia. Convulsions threatened. Mr. Burton waited here to lunch, and for some hours. A highly gentlemanly person and pecu-

liarly clever with children." "Lady Goding Goding recommended me to try the 'Sister of Mercy for the Nursery,' a new soothing compound for little Albert. I got some from Corbyn, and Swanston tells me it stops his worst fits, and she seems to like it. She is a very experienced and valuable nurse." Next day I find:—
"I happened to mention to Burton that we were using the 'Sister of Mercy for the Nursery,' and he was *horrified!* He said it was a morphitic drug! of a *highly detrimental* nature, sometimes producing idiocy!! I threw the bottle into the fire, and gave Swanston a sound rating for not knowing better than to administer poison to a child. I am seriously thinking of looking out for another nurse. It is positively frightful to think of his taking any incentive to idiocy."—"Little Albert has a *tooth!* I can just see a white line in the lower gum," etc., etc., etc., etc. Then he walked, then he talked, then he grew, then he fell into his hot-water bath before the cold had been added, and for a while his head was denuded of its objectionable orange attachments. This accident led to the extradition of poor Swanston, who happened to be absent from the room at the time, a fact of which her maid was taking advantage to signal out of the window to a groom in the mews behind.

Why do I transcribe these frivolous items? Not certainly to induce a smile at Lady Ffowlsmere's expense, who, God bless her, was writing so far as her child was concerned the petty details of a large and honest affection; proving herself natural indeed, spite of philosophy, politics and position. Yet I would have you note the weakness there was in that love and estimate of her child which was biassed enough to overpower the sense of justice to others: how unconsciously selfish, foolish and unfair a woman may be in the strength of maternal affection and the arrogance of class superiority: further, how extreme a contrast you may draw between the minute anxiety, the lavish carefulness bestowed upon this infant compatriot, and the dubious, cursory, nay injurious disregard, whereof many a sad young immortal in these rich islands is a daily martyr. The satirist who turns his glass upon these discrepancies of humanity executes no willing task if he be a true man, yet most certainly is discharging a public duty. We need throughout society a wider recognition of human equality, not in condition, but in right and spirit. In the high latitudes of aristocratic birth and breeding, I for one grudge no little lord or lady devoted kindness and all the minute luxurious comfort money can secure. But let them not congratulate themselves that this is more than circumstance or that it confers a right to qualify the rights of others. The egotism of class is a danger impregnate with bitter seeds. It is fostered at the expense of that broad humanity which seeking finds on every hand some chain of sympathy with those around it—which recognises a duty rising above self and reaching also downwards to the very depths of brother-nature. The prejudices based in this assumption corrupt even still the principles of legislation and the roots of society. *Title* is made a term of substance, not of relation ; *vested interests* are accepted as a justification for the intolerable; *property* is looked upon as a thing of right and not of trust : *superiority*, even in its relation to social status, a fallacious and impudent assumption, is made the ground of an unequal distribution of power and the inequitable administration of justice. No marvel if the man who suffers from these brilliant impostures of society, who is sensible how much they impede the fine sweep of free principles, should sometimes turn with a sort of horrified resignation to FORCE as the only solvent of conditions too hard to be longer endured !

You, who in exalted places, have in your pure souls struggled successfully against the blinding vanity of class are heroes and heroines whom I reverence,—for your temptation is not such as is common to man.

III.—Academic Groves.

AT this period of our hero's life, the affairs of his elder brother Lord Bantam began to attract the painful attention of his father, as they had for some time acquired a curious notoriety out of doors. The Earl brought up his heir as he had himself been reared. He restricted him to a small allowance, and urged him, as a matter of habit, to maintain over his expenditure a rigid control. Then he sent him to Winton. There Lord Bantam repaid the advice he had received by incurring debts to the extent of £3,000. His creditors were too glad to have such a debtor, and too clever to let out the young nobleman's secrets. So his father knew nothing of them, and supposed that he had managed well on his allowance of £100 a year. These debts were running on at thirty per cent. interest compounded every three months. From Winton he went to Camford.

Camford to visit is a charming place; it seems to breathe of quiet, of patient monastic study and noble wisdom-bearing silence. Its grey stones are as if strewn with the hoar of antique and classic pedantry. As you pass through its groined passages, traverse its cloistered quadrangles, survey its stately halls or worship in its venerable churches, you think that here at least learning has found her proper seat; sequestered from the rough passions of the world, secure from the intrusion of vanity and debauch, silent with Herself, Her duty, and Her God. It ought to be so, but it is not. I know not why it should not be. The passage through those splendid portals no gold should buy, no rank should gain. It should, with all the honours and comforts of the noble foundations, be free to any son of England who has the wit and worth to win the right. Surely you should shut from thence your maudlin or your fool, your *roué*, your turfman, your fashionable lounger, whatever his name or estate; and open these serious gates alone to the sons of work and thought and duty. As it is, in this rank soil many a promising grain of wheat is choked and smothered amidst the strong growths of folly and sin, while the husbandmen look on, their hands too idle or too craven to weed them out.

Depend upon it, you select company of ecclesiastics, dons and tutors, if you do not set about this reform yourselves, a healthy tide from without will sweep into and around your cosy haven and drift you out to perdition with the foul wreck you have permitted to accumulate about you.

IV.—A young Aristocrat.

To Camford went Lord Bantam. Its trading harpies hastened to offer to so good a customer every facility for ruining himself. He accepted their kind offices. Never even in that luxurious place were rooms so handsomely furnished, horses so good, traps so elegant, dinners and wines so expensive, pictures so costly, and women so fast as those of Lord Bantam's establishments in High Church and the town. Much of this was notorious throughout the university, and must have been as patent to some of the dons as to the gossips in High

Street. But they made no protest, except when the noble undergraduate came under proctorial notice in a drunken row; and once, when he and a few select companions had contrived to enter the cathedral at night, and colour a fine marble with lines in zebra-fashion, they expelled two of his accomplices who were so unfortunate as to have no titled name to dishonour; forced the young gentleman to apologise, and wrote to the Earl that "a recurrence of such conduct might lead to the most serious consequences." The syndicate must have had a curious notion of education. They could hardly have believed that the spectacle of folly and prodigality was innocuous to university tone and discipline! Is it theirs only to open their eyes to deficiences in ecclesiastical, classical, and philosophic acquirements, and to shut them to the extravagance and sin of the alumni? or were it not a chiefest part of education to teach the lessons of high humanity—*ingenuae et humanae artes?* Should it be possible for any pupil at a seat of learning to emulate the vices of Commodus, or ought not sumptuary laws to confine the rivalry of prodigals within bounds less perilous to studious moralities?

Of a morning, towards noon, a quadrangle hard by the great cathedral rang with loud voices. Perched upon his window-sill, velvet-capped, with pewter in hand, Lord Bantam held spicy converse with the son of a prime minister who leaned smoking out of an opposite casement, or exchanged bets and jokes of a dubious character with a knot of noisy men on the pavement below. You, an honest Englishman, wishing well for your country, and having a kindly heart for manly and generous youth, might well wonder as you traversed the court and gazed upon this scene, whether idle nobility and parvenu wealth should be afforded in the precincts of hallowed shrines and the cloisters of learning, footholds to corrupt the hopes of coming generations.

Lord Bantam's expenses, his first year at Camford, were £15,000; he owed £11,000 to money-lenders on his own notes and those of his friends. His father's steward had managed to get him allowed £4,000. His tailor stood creditor for £3,000. That clever gentleman did not confine his shears to cutting cloth, he snipped off many a young man's income with a sharpness and skill sometimes wanting in his proper work. He charged young Bantam in his bill with clothes and jewellery never supplied; and thus, on condition of sharing the product, enabled him to cheat his father. The noble youth began to evince a taste for the turf. He won the High Church sweepstakes for the Derby—in which by-the-way several dons had their money—amounting to "800 sovs"—as at Winton, under the noses of the masters, he had won a school sweepstakes before. He picked up a shrewd gambler named Tom Rendle, made him his factotum, and in his name bought and ran his horses. At first they were successful. He resolved to have stables of his own. Rendle was an admirable factotum. He found the money, the horses, the stables, the jockeys, took sheaves of notes, negotiated them with innocent friends, and never troubled his master with accounts. He looked upon the young lord as the richest mine in England for a clever man. All this was concealed from the Earl, who, engrossed in politics and Rotterdam riches, knew little of racing matters, would not have known his son's colours if he had seen them; and society does not care to tattle the peccadillos of a coming star to a noble statesman. When he came of age Lord Bantam owed £40,000. By the end of that year his liabilities reached £95,000, and in two years more were £200,000. He had of course left Camford, and had his secret nests about the country; formed liaison after liaison with masculine indifference to the other sex; and at length fell into the net of an infinitely clever beauty, provided along with the other animals by the attentive Rendle. This person was now a gentleman, a "financier," who kept his carriage and gave select dinners to the princes of the turf. The woman was his slave. She pretended that Lord Bantam had seduced her. He was infatuated with her almost to idiocy. She threatened to expose him to the Earl, was backed up by Rendle, and the pair keeping their game for a fortnight in a state of alternate drunkenness, maudlinism and fear,—at length succeeded in getting him to marry her. Returning from the unholy ceremony as with a blast upon him from the shrine he had profaned; wedded in delirium and never recognising his infamous wife—

* * * *
* * * * * *
* * * * * *
* * * * * *

Does any one ask whether it be true that a thing so horrible could happen in England in these days?

The Earl paid his son's debts like an Earl; after all they did not absorb a year's income; and not long after the factotum married Lady Bantam.

Thus at four years old our hero became Lord Bantam, and it was fortunate for him that he was too young to know the scandal he inherited with the name. It was a scandal of a sort whereof society does not make more than a nine days' wonder. There is great repairing power in an Earldom and several hundred thousands a year.

PART III.

HOW HE LEARNED HIS LETTERS.

I.—Words versus Wit.

EARL FFOWLSMERE was so distraught at the hapless fate of his elder son that he shrank from sending our hero to Winton. He therefore provided tutors at home. No doubt this had a peculiar influence on the young lord's future character. It deprived him of a society in which he would have found rank, prospects and good breeding on a par with his own, yet not unduly asserting themselves over less fortunate accidents. He might also have acquired a considerable skill in writing verses in languages hardly an Englishman would venture to attempt to speak, a quantity of valuable aphorisms for quotation in his future elevated sphere, a crude idea of English, an ingeniously bad hand-writing, and probably some proficiency in cricket and rowing. The curriculum would not have afforded him much more, unless indeed we include an acquisition, perforce of continued iteration, of certain prayers, psalms and lessons of the Church. At home, if he were deprived of the companionship and the sports and the finished elegance of classic composition, his range of acquisition went deeper into the well of knowledge and wider over its fields. He was taught French and German by conversation. He learned his Latin to speak it, not neglecting the verses as trifles contributing to polish his style. A scientific German tutor opened to him the rich veins of natural science, and laid the foundation for some knowledge of the world about him. The Earl himself took in hand historical instruction, conveyed more by conversation and illustration than by tasks, seeking to indoctrinate him as he advanced from boyhood with his own political ideas and a reverence for the British Constitution. This latter teaching afterwards refuted its own purpose; for the youth, as we shall see, did not accept with perfect faith the political theses of the statesman. The Earl was particularly eager that his son should be "a speaker." Recognising the power of talk in modern representative systems, he desired that the future Earl should be versed in all its clever and seductive tricks. Almost before he had emerged from boyhood he trained him in elocution; he set him to declaim the orations of ancient and modern masters: he drilled him in Quintilian. Adopting the example of Lord Chatham with his son, he put him to translate extempore from classic authors: finally, he announced to him topics for off-hand speeches. Hence at fifteen, when Lord Bantam went to Oxbridge, he was a ready speaker, and took his place at the Union among its chief debaters. Whether this facility of utterance was given at the expense of better acquirements may hereafter appear; at present we may mention it procured for our hero the sobriquet of "Crowing Bantam." If sobriquets were only fatal, one would hope that such an one might be attached to not a few of our parliamentarian orators. It is conceivable that the ensuing mortality might be a wholesome thing for the State.

II.—Digression. Benevolently dedicated to American Readers.

I HAVE seen occasional suggestions in the press that on this branch of education it would be well to assimilate our system to that of America. But, if there is a root of wisdom in the hint, there are also roots of evil. Mr. Carlyle has embodied in language too vigorous and noble to be emulated his protest against present-day chatter, and one may only very diffidently say a word or two on the matter in its relation to education. In the United States the culture of speech-making begins almost before the culture of thought. Indeed not long after a few words and ideas have found some lodgment in a young mind, they are casually and cursorily shaken up within it by the demand for "an oration" on some impossible thesis. Fact and history are necessarily awanting to such juvenile spouters, wherefore they are forced to concoct their exercitations partly from imagination and partly from imperfect data. They are encouraged to be theorists before they become cognisant of truths. So universal is the Yankee propensity to orationizing, that to it must be attributed in no small degree the singularly metaphysical and theoretic character of ordinary American reasoning, even on the commonest matters of social or political life; still more those rare and monstrous forms of argument they sometimes advance in international negotiation. You find your neighbour at a dinner-table, in defiance of Baconian maxims, elaborately generalising from one particular. No people in the world has equal talent for the ornamental expression of nothing. Tracing the effect of this on all popular thought, all popular opinion, all popular action,—it is to substitute "smartness" for learning—plausibility for fact—to dissolve instead of to crystallise truth in words. Few Americans estimate a word at its correct value. Few of them seem to feel it to be a precious thing not to be squandered: not to be abused to set untruth or commonplace or unreality: a thing which wielded with exactness and care carries in it a glorious might, but which thrown out with slovenly or shallow incaution is a folly or a sin. To be ready in expressing the results of study and thought is a faculty of faculties: to cover with thin and melting flakes of eloquence an underground of ignorance, is to spread delusion for the weakest and most numerous of mankind.

III.—A juvenile Tourist and Author.

Our hero having safely passed the measles reached the comparatively mature age of twelve years. "Comparatively" with all the children and most of the adults that were huddled together in the murky mews and alleys over which he looked from his high schoolroom windows. Mature in things they recked not of—a reader, a speaker of French with a touch of German, advanced in Latin : deft at composing elegant nonsense lyrics : a juvenile mathematician : learned in Bible and Catechism ; familiar with that skeleton of the past called history.

He could also cut a tolerable figure in a drawing-room, make a neat bow, and give an opinion with sufficient aristocratic confidence. In other matters comparison finds him unequal to his hapless compatriots. In forward shrewdness, cat-like cunning, ready-resource, bold defiance of law and cool irrecognition of Gospel, in early precocity of talent for business, he was necessarily inferior to his inferiors. As nature had imperfectly constructed him for fighting, he would also have taken a mean place in an alley scrimmage.

Is there no drawing these two extremes nearer together, the one up the other down? Is it the inevitable predestination of the Almighty that the young Lord Bantam shall be and dwell thus: and the child of Ginx shall be and dwell so—Lazarus and Dives, with a great gulf fixed between them?

At this stage of their son's life the Earl and Countess resolved upon passing some months at various Courts on the continent. Like the meteors their movements were chronicled in the newspapers, and gave rise to grave conjectures that they had gone abroad on some political mission. From Paris the correspondent of the *Electro Magnet* wrote the startling information that he "had met the Earl at a *petit déjeûner* of three, in a certain Imperial sanctum, where secrets had transpired which mortal might not utter; but he might say, without breaking any confidence, that the world would, in the course of three weeks or so, hear news that would rouse Empires and disturb the equilibrium of centuries."

The result was a confidential despatch from Berlin to the Prussian ambassador in London, instructing him to ascertain if possible what secret mission was sending the Earl and Countess of Ffowlsmere intriguing in half the Courts of Europe. The ambassador's reply was as sarcastic as it was reassuring. He informed his Government that "he had lived long enough in England to learn that its diplomacy proceeded not by intrigue but by blunders: that it was impossible to suppose his excellent and mediocre friend the Earl of Ffowlsmere to be engaged, either of his own motion or by direction of the British Government, in any diplomatic mission: that, as to the Government, it was the English custom to declare its objects beforehand: and even if the report were true, he was sure no harm could come of it to any nation but England herself, since the avowed course of English policy—by which the Earl must necessarily be restricted—was to disown anything but peace and its result—money; and to play for plausible if sometimes undignified releases from inconvenient obligations."

Young Bantam with his tutor accompanied this distinguished party from London to Paris: from Paris to Vienna: from Vienna to the Danubian Provinces: to Constantinople, Athens, and Rome. He was observant, was well primed by his tutor, conversed with his father on elementary politics, and was petted by Princes who desired to maintain good relations with England. He received the Pope's benediction. As with other young persons, when his mind began to work it became eager to afford visible evidence thereof; so the young lord wrote a book. It is the fashion now-a-days for youthful lords, baronets, and gentlemen of wealth to make grand tours in out-of-the-way regions, and to record their hasty observations and necessarily limited generalisations in books that not many years afterwards they are glad if others are as willing to forget as themselves.

"The Danubian Provinces: with Notes Social and Statistical: by Lord Bantam," was not the worst of such productions I have seen. It related very simply what he had experienced; recorded opinions founded on facts; and being written by an Earl's son, and to be had at all the libraries, could not fail to gain a temporary notoriety in middle-class drawing-rooms. I may select a specimen from the chapter on "Rowmania."

"Lord F—— and I went to call upon the Prince of Rowmania. He did not look like a Prince. He was bandy-legged. I did not wonder therefore when I was told that his people did not like him. While he was talking to papa he said he was a good deal on horseback. He also said he had to keep horses saddled day and night, because every few weeks there was a revolution, and he had to ride away for his life. I asked him why he did not cut off the heads of the people who rebelled. He said that if he were to that he would have no subjects left. It struck me on the other hand, that it would be better to do that than to have one's own head cut off: and my father said 'there were precedents for that opinion of a ruler's duty to himself.' Coming away, another remark of Lord F—— particularly struck me: namely, 'that it was a wonder any one should persist in trying to govern when it was so plain his efforts were unsatisfactory to the people: but that the ambition of ruling often makes men insensible to its absurdities.'"

Simple as were young Bantam's observations, there was found to be an unconscious satirical flavour about them which one or two clever journalists utilised for home application.

IV.—A Scotch Tutor.

ONE of the tutors engaged for Lord Bantam was a Mr. Kelso, a Scotchman, who had been strongly recommended to the Earl. The latter and his lady both hesitated about bringing the young heir into contact with a man whom they expected to be imbued with the religious views of the Presbyterians—but on the other hand, they had reason to believe that his ability and morality were unexceptionable. It turned out that this gentleman had been educated at a Scotch University, and had undergone the necessary studies to fit him for the ministry of the Scotch Church. In the course of his reading—he was omnivorous in books—he struck out for himself some lines of thought not quite consistent with the interpretation put by his Church Courts upon the Confession of Faith. Hence when he came to apply to the Presbytery to license him as a preacher, and to submit himself for the necessary examination, it was discovered that on some points of doctrine he was "unsound." He was not quite clear about the legal obligation of the Sabbath, though he admitted it to be practically enjoined on his conscience. This was hinted to the Presbytery by some ready officer, and without proof that his heterodoxy was heinous, a vote consigned him to perpetual laity, so far as that Church was concerned. I have nothing at this moment to do with the merits of the objections—but I have to do with the fact that they drove into opposition a man whom perhaps a little kindliness would have brought either to abjure his errors or to show that he had none. As it was, he left with a sense of injury that rankled deeply in his breast, and he looked upon the rejectors as a lot of unconscientious bigots, which they really never meant to be.

We have the measure of Lord Bantam's grounding in the faith. He had been taught with some rigour the truths of the Christian religion and the formulas of his Church. He could state them all with tolerable readiness and exactness—so far as words went. They were not however crystallised in his life. But then he had been taught to be afraid not to believe, instead of to believe and not be afraid. There could hardly therefore be much groundwork of faith.

No doubt the Earl and Countess would have been deeply and sincerely resentful had any one suggested a question of their religiousness. Were they not extremely precise in their conduct? honourable and sensitive in their motives? sufficiently attentive to the ritual of their Church? Was there any voice so firm as the Earl's, so decorously reverent as that of the Countess in the responses to the service? Did they not with regularity receive the sacrament of Communion? Were not all forms of heresy equally odious to them—whether it were Erastian or Roman or Arian or Socinian? Yet it may be that in their deep probing of other things, the noble pair had but scratched the surface of true religion. This is a matter irrespective of the mere substance of belief. A religion, in its integrity, whatever a man may believe, is that which informs and *possesses* his soul and rules with despotic sway his whole life. You could scarcely say that of the high-bred consent accorded by Lord and Lady Ffowlsmere to a supremely respectable form of Church doctrine and ritual. You may test it, if you please, by their conduct respecting young Bantam. They brought him up as they themselves had been brought up. He was duly catechised, the Earl himself not disdaining to overlook so important a business. He went to church and attended morning prayers as regularly as the Earl's servants—and with equally good results. He was warned of sundry deadly sins, which however it seemed to be as much a part of gentility as of religion to avoid. He heard continually expressed and saw repeatedly exhibited his parents' abhorrence of all manner of meanness, blasphemy, impropriety and heresy. But nothing he heard or saw or was taught went down to the roots of his nature, and that is the very part of a man where true religion begins to work, and thence like nourishment to a tree flows up in wealthy sap, carrying strength and life, and greenness, and fruitfulness through the whole being. To sum up the result of his religious discipline, it taught him to be moral and reverential—but not to be religious. He learned to respect the Church, but was not quite so fixed in his affection for God—a Deity who loves his creatures, and whom it becomes them ingenuously to love. That was presented to his mind as an Entity too awful and sequestered to be a subject of common thought.

Yet there is a noble passage in the preaching of a noble Apostle—which says that God is not far from any one of us; and it seems to me that the Church or the creed or the ritual or the dogma that intervenes with a screen, however beautiful and elaborate, between me panting for a parent's love and daily familiarity, and the parent yearning for my childlike affection, is a barrier to be swept away, unless it will of itself open up to show me more clearly the vision and fruition of that divine joy.

His first tutor, a former Testminster man, had followed with his pupil the course prescribed in that celebrated school, and had carefully conveyed through the chilling winter climate of "Pearson on the Creed," a mind just budding into its young spring life, and unequal to the cold hardness of the metaphysic; before it had learned to appreciate the practical bearings on his daily actions of religious and moral principles. To touch his heart, to reach his conscience, to awaken his most generous sentiments, to prompt his aspirations after all things pure, noble, virtuous, honest, of good report, to raise his thoughts to God as his Creator, Redeemer and Friend, —all this was made secondary—though not entirely forgotten—to defining in his mind a strict outline of dogmas, the truth or untruth of which matters not in this relation. The more truthful, the greater the impolicy of pressing them in this hard form and at this stage of growth, on a fledgling mind.

Bantam became very fond of his Scotch tutor. There was something attractive in the man's peculiar shrewdness and tenacity of intellect, the breadth and comprehensiveness of his views of every topic, the enormous store of material which loving and incessant study had accumulated in his mind.

The quaint humour, the genial tenderness of sympathy, the half-worshipping appreciation of great men and great words: the reverence and piety, along with the strange cold dogmatism of much of his belief; the whole tempered by the charity, not so much of principle as of a loving nature, made a character not uncommon in Scotland, and perhaps agreeable only to a select few. From this man the young lord learned many heresies. Kelso had read history as men seldom read it, with a broad apprehension of movements and results which gave to his conclusions peculiar force and splendour. He tracked with keen scent the course of liberty in the communities of Greece, in Rome, through the Dark Ages; took up the double thread of her movement in religious and political combination at the Reformation, and showed how Bible principles, and Bible forms of thought, and the subtle puissant influences of Christ's wonderful teaching had helped to dissolve the ancient forces of society, had even marked the outlines of modern liberalism and aided in modifying forms of government. To the Puritan or Presbyterian element he showed how much of modern republican and democratic sentiment was due, based as its ecclesiastical organization had always been on the recognition for the laity of freedom of thought and equality of representation in Church government. He showed how this, backed by a strangely firm faith in a few great dogmas, had worked with almost invincible power, and so always must work when such an organization is true to its principles and itself. Bantam, whose vague young notions had exalted episcopacy to almost divine establishment, began to believe that it and the monarchical and aristocratic institutions of his country all stood on the same basis, human invention—lived only on the same condition—human patience; and that there was good reason to doubt if any or all of these vast institutions would bear criticism in the light of truth or Christianity, of experience or even of common sense. Instead of feeling proud of his lineage, his wealth and his religion, he was led to question the honour of the one, the justice of the other, and the purity of the third.

At the same time Mr. Kelso pointed out to him how much good there was in each.

Specially did Kelso protest to his young charge against the creed-worship of the day. "A creed," he used to say, "is a declaration of faith; it ought to be the crystallisation in words of a man's soul-thoughts and faith, the outlines of his daily life with God. In fact the best creed I know is the Beatitudes. They embody practical belief. But simply accepted from another man, adopted in terror, and held under the threats of a terrible sanction —not grasped and brought into the soul, and incorporated with its life—a creed is only a semblance; it is 'Nehushtan:' *stuff*, not life. Strauss used to begin one of his lectures by saying, 'Gentlemen, we will now proceed to construct God.' He was not more profane than many a man who shrinks from his profanity. I have often thought, when I have seen men going about to construct creeds, or limning out for themselves God's features and decrees, in their own words and ideas, of Isaiah's scornful satire on the wooden-god makers of his day :—

The carpenter stretcheth out *his* rule; he marketh it out with a line; he fitteth it with planes, and he marketh it out with the compass, and maketh it after the figure of a man, according to the beauty of a man; that it may remain in the house.

He heweth him down cedars, and taketh the cypress and the oak, which he strengeneth for himself among the trees of the forest: he planteth an ash, and the rain doth nourish *it*.

Then shall it be for a man to burn : for he shall take thereof and warm himself; yea, he kindleth *it*, and baketh bread; yea, he maketh a god, and worshippeth *it*: he maketh it a graven image, and falleth down thereto.

He burneth part thereof in the fire; with part thereof he eateth flesh; he roasteth roast, and is satisfied: yea, he warmeth *himself*, and saith, Aha, I am warm, I have seen the fire:

And the residue thereof he maketh a god, *even* his graven image: he falleth down unto it, and worshippeth *it*, and prayeth unto it, and saith, Deliver me; for thou *art* my god.

"What cutting ridicule, what a sarcastic rebuke of man's assumption! And there is little difference between *wood* and *words*. From both you may make your idols: your fetish may be one of sentences. Unless we bow reverently before God, own our ignorance and his omniscience, humbly and contritely wait upon the high and lofty One who inhabiteth eternity, till He condescends to invision with Himself the lowly spirit—unless we will permit God to declare Himself, instead of ourselves constructing Him, we can have no genuine insight into His being or into our relations to Him."

Kelso's secular teaching was equally broad; and I am not prepared to exonerate him from blame for taking advantage of his position to instil such ideas into the mind of a young lord, already red headed and vaccinated with Radical lymph. The tutor's views were singularly unlike those of the Prigs.

"Look," said he, "at the way in which the high business of our government is now carried on. Can you pick out a single statesman who looks beyond the limits of the present, or the narrow circuit of these islands, or who takes any broad, practical view of the Imperial future? One only of them all has uttered a timorous squeak about a great confederation of English-speaking peoples; but from the rest, on the destinies of Empire, we have had nothing but dead silence, or twitterings about cost and policy, as abject, narrow and disloyal as they were perilous. As yet no man of them has propounded, in noble, heart-stirring, vivid language, the idea of an united Britain—not the isolated nodules of these petty isles, but the far-stretching Imperial boulder of a third of the globe. The grand effort of organizing the *disjecta membra* of this enormous dominion into a concrete federation appals men bent on conciliating Irish irreconcilables with Westmeath commissions, and the truncheons of policemen or the cutlasses and revolvers of a constabulary.

"Let us look at home. Take the conditions of our society. See the labouring classes seething and uneasy, feeling the pressure of a yoke they cannot define, though it is hard as iron; restless for remedies they know not how to invent: conscious only, and rightly conscious, that their state is not what God meant it to be, nor what, in the face of man, it ought to be, nor what, by the help of God to the contrary, they intend it shall be. Where is the statesman who seems to appreciate the perils of the hour—who, by temperate and judicious handling of the body politic, will attempt to facilitate the readjustment of the disproportioned or disjointed members, and set it fairly on its four feet? The Commune flourishes on the antagonism of the economists—living logic of facts against dead logic of principle. Is there no God-ordained statesman to see that vents must be found for the pent-up forces of society, or that the inevitable explosion of fierce, petrolous horror will shatter it again to a chaos of primitive atoms? Let us be sure of one thing —sure as the sun shines, sure as God's existence—such a man must rise, must lead the people of these realms in the direction of reforms now scouted by the self-inspired so-called *economic* seers, shining newspaper demi-gods and Idol Statesmen, or Inferno itself will come up through the ground, and spread its horrors over this fair England. Happy for us that, from time to time, such vents have been found in Reform Bills, in emancipation from religious bondage, in Free Corn, and Free Trade; but now these have largely worked out their remedy, society is getting clogged again, and the voice of resistless human progress shouts for more. Do you think you can stop it with doctrinaire objections? Do you think you can choke it with political sugar-plums, with the ballot, with half-concessions to trades unions, nay, even if you grant education? This education will be the lever which must upheave the very foundations of our present society. Will the Nehushtans of monarchy, of State-Church, of House of Peers and hereditary successions, of Land Monopolisers, Charitable Corporations, Bumbledoms, stand when that huge lever, worked by twenty millions, is brought to bear upon them? Never!

Hence the man who would see these ancient tenements gradually and securely taken to pieces, not shattering down with blood and terror on their hapless inhabitants, will wisely commence his reforms now, lest the tower of Siloam prove a grave to many not unrighteous persons. We must recognise the fact at once, that society, which means the State, has more to do than register the occurrence of politico-economic facts : it must grasp and deal with the evils of the community in a spirit of politic generosity. The spirit of legislation must be transformed. Revolutionary remedies are not necessary. They may by judicious foresight be prevented. The coming struggle is between *laissez-faire* and that almost equally bad and perilous socialism which looks to the State to do everything. Between these two lies the happy mean. The State cannot refuse to take its part in its own reorganization; the people must do their part in their own improvement. You are shut in with them ; you must face them and their demands ; you must admit their difficulties, disabilities, distresses ; you must concede to them that you owe them more than the duty of paying some imperfect *quid pro quo;* you must find out some way of distributing more equally the plethoric wealth of these kingdoms amongst its people—or prepare for the deluge. Even the ancient Spanish family that had an ark of its own in Noah's inundation would be hard bestead to find anything that would float above this one."

Another time he spoke in a somewhat similar strain:—

"Make the best of your day. Your class and wealth distinction is one that your grandchild may not see. This is a rapid era. The strata of society that hitherto have looked so solid and fixed give signs of volcanic motion. The aristocratic layer of our constitution is swiftly, daily becoming inconsistent with the rising power and forces of society. There are two methods of convulsion: either the lowest stratum will be upheaved with terrific force, and bursting through the others come up at last to the surface through the old red sandstone of feudocracy; or it is just possible that such a fortunate convulsion may take place as you can see in a bay in the Isle of Wight, where all the strata have risen together and stand almost perpendicular, side by side, mutually supporting, no one above another. Much depends on the upper stratum. If it is thick and inflexible, it will be split and shivered by the lower upheaving forces. The feudal system has been decaying with the growth of English liberty—which like ivy has spread and flourished over its crumbling glories. Relics still remain, but they are incompatible with the changes that have been wrought in our social ideas and political bases; they must give way, and your class gives way with them. It will be the last to give way, because of the vitality constantly imported into it from the middle classes. But two dangers menace it. One danger is the weakness, ignorance or folly of the class itself. The other is the breaking down of its main tower, the monarchy. An unpopular monarch will not only commit suicide for the royalty of England, but will carry with him to extinction the fabric of aristocracy. Possibly the former will be the method of disaster to the most concrete anomaly of modern constitutions—an aristocracy based on feudal fictions, existing on popular sufferance, and maintained only by the fortuitous dignity and sagacity of its members. You must see that such a patent incongruity cannot long brave the criticism of political philosophy or the selfish keenness of vulgar instinct."

V.—Catholicism.

ONE peculiar phase of Mr. Kelso's teaching, afterwards exercised on Lord Bantam's opinions a permanent influence.

The tutor might boast of a broad experience of "churches." As a student for the ministry he had been at various times utilized by Wesleyans, Baptists, Primitives, and Independents: he had preached for Morrisonians, Burghers, Anti-burghers, Old Lights and New Lights—and Plymouth Brethren. Of each and all he could sharply expose the weaknesses; but of every one he also held some approving opinion. He endeavoured to convey to his pupil the lesson he had himself learned from this unique intercourse with the sects; namely, that while there was much in each that was grotesque,—while every one of them needed apology, reform and "the gift of charity,"—there was not one in which might not be found many good points. In his view, each of these sects had a great deal to learn from the others. His comprehensive acquaintance with them enabled him also to illustrate the fact, that many of the matters wherein they were most viciously antagonistic were those that appeared to be the least relevant to a broad and true religion.

"You see," said Kelso, one day, "religion ought to be adaptive. If it were not so it could not be universal, and no religion not fitted to become universal can be a true religion. It is impossible to conceive of so unreasonable a thing as a religion to be true when appropriate only to a fraction of mankind. The Christian religion alone, in its purity, answers to that test. It meets all natures and all circumstances and all times. Hence you observe its various aspects. With some people it assumes the form of an intellectual adoption of principles with rigid adherence to regulations. In other cases, it is a matter of emotion or even passion, and plays upon its subjects with strange and almost grotesque influences. With some it is a soft spiritual influence transfusing the life—to others a rough series of struggles, with their alternating hopes and despair. Endless modifications naturally result; but after all you will find at the bottom of many of them the same facts, the same ideas, producing the various developments of religious feeling, action, form,—and that the greatest apparent discrepancies are incrustations on a pure and common ideal. I now disregard these incrustations, and with difficulty, but I hope with success, seek this pure basis. I can worship with almost any sect of Christians, since I can disregard the accidents and agree in the substance."

"I have never seen any religious ceremonies other than those of our own Church," said young Bantam, "and am curious to know the distinctions in ritual and manner between the various denominations."

"That," said Kelso, "would undoubtedly be useful to you. Many of the prejudices maintained between opposing sects would melt away or be qualified by more intimate contact with them. I have been often struck with the ignorance displayed by polemical disputants of the real practice and belief of their antagonists. In many cases, no doubt, a hopeless want of human sympathy or a dishonest indifference prevents men from acquiring such knowledge."

They agreed to visit some of the dissenting chapels, and, as a specimen of their experiences, it is necessary that I should describe the first introduction of the young aristocrat and churchman to an unfamiliar phase of Protestantism.

One day the tutor and his pupil, in the course of a long walk from Shufflestraw Castle, returning through the town of Ffowlsmere, noticed a placard on an obscure chapel of the sort that sometimes crouch in the neighbourhood of old town churches. It announced that the Reverend Dr. Roper, a famous leader among the Primitive Christians, would preach at a certain service to be held in the chapel on the succeeding evening, and that after the service a love-feast would be held.

Kelso seized the opportunity.

"You cannot do better than go to this," said he, "I have heard this man, who really has a great deal of originality, and the 'love-feast' is sure to acquaint you with an interesting phase of enthusiasm."

Accordingly, the next evening, the two slipped away from the castle. The chapel was a rectangular structure of brick, with a false pediment of the same material. On the frieze below it, in stucco letters, were the words,

MIZPAH.

1789.

Within, it presented an array of high narrow pews on the floor, galleries supported on wooden columns, which exhibited an alarming tendency to bulge, and a pulpit in shape having the appearance of a red mahogany tulip exalted on a very inadequate stem. To this a serpentine staircase afforded access. Entering the gallery the gentlemen found that the seats seemed designed to prove that purgatory might exist on earth and therefore need not to be looked for half way to heaven. But the people appeared unconscious of discomfort. They were of a class somewhat novel to the church-going young lord: many women, tradespeople, small farmers, labourers and domestics. Some of them had walked ten or twelve miles to hear the preacher, and would afterwards walk home again without grumbling. As Lord Bantam looked round, he observed a freedom of demeanour, which indicated that for them the place itself had no special sacredness.

Some talked, one or two men retained their hats, but a few seemed to be engaged in silent prayer. Presently a small door behind the pulpit opened, and two or three persons came out; one a short, stout man, with a round face, straight black hair and a large mouth, his white, expansive and untidy necktie designating the preacher of the day. The others were clearly official brethren of some weight in the community, amongst whom Lord Bantam recognised the principal grocer of Ffowlsmere.

Instant silence fell upon the congregation as the heavy-looking minister slowly laboured up the cork-screw staircase to the pulpit, holding the rails in either hand, and creaking the steps with his weight as he went. Once up and shut sharply into the tulip by the attendant, he knelt in prayer, and on rising opened the book before him and gave out a hymn. When he had read the hymn through, he re-read the first two lines. A pause ensued. It was clear the musical resources of the meeting were limited. The minister looked round calmly and said:—

"Is there no one who can raise the tune?"

Lord Bantam smiled, but a whisper from Kelso warned him not to allow his own sense of ritual decorum to warp his judgment.

"This is unusual to you," said he; "but nothing really absurd has happened as yet. With these people, you see, religion is quite an *at home* affair."

No one seemed inclined to "start the tune," whereupon in a cheery voice the minister himself led off to a jolly air, which was instantly taken up with spirit by the whole congregation, Lord Bantam finding himself irresistibly drawn into the performance. After reading a lesson from Scripture, Dr. Roper knelt down, and waiting a few seconds for the establishment of perfect stillness, began in a low, well-managed tone, a prayer that seemed to strike and thrill through every fibre of the people's hearts. He appeared to have forgotten everything but the Maker above and the creatures below—the majesty of the one, the abjectness of the other; and as one or other idea came uppermost in his mind, his voice rose and rang like a war-shout, or fell into the whisper of penitential sorrow and entreaty. Young Bantam had often heard the Bishop of Dunshire animadvert on the irregular extempore exercitations of sectaries, but as his eyes shot down the eager drops upon the floor, he bore witness to a power which, whatever its cause, had never been present to him elsewhere. One peculiarity about it was, however, obnoxious to the young man. The

Doctor was praying, but he was also preaching. Every now and then his doctrine came out in some strong, sharp proposition which prefaced its appropriate entreaty.

"We know, O God, that Thou art a Judge—terrible in Thy power! inflexible in Thy justice! that to be consistent with Thyself Thou must and wilt punish the wicked. Yet, how merciful Thou art! providing a Saviour in Christ: and here are sinners before Thee— men and women lost in sin, who have never sought Thee, who know not the love of Jesus, who have not found peace in their Saviour, who have not realised the power of His redeeming blood, who have not put on the robes of His righteousness: they are dead in trespasses and sins, they are lost to grace, they descend the paths of destruction. Hell opens its mouth unto them with eternal fires—O God of mercy, have mercy, and

"'—snatch them from the burning grave!'"

The congregation grew gradually excited, the occasional "amens" gave place to fervent and repeated exclamations from all parts of the building. A low wail here and there showed some conscience-stricken soul to be giving vent to its feelings, and Lord Bantam began to feel it too painful to be endured. At length the man ceased, and changing his tone rapidly repeated the Lord's Prayer. As he ended, a great sigh went up from the people, and a general movement for a few moments delayed the service. The minister stood wiping the beads from his face. He had been having a strong wrestle with Satan. Moved as Bantam was, he thought all this in shockingly bad taste, but he began nevertheless to have a respect for the preacher. After another hymn had been sung, Dr. Roper announced his text: " It is a faithful saying, and worthy of all acceptation, that Christ Jesus came into the world to save sinners."

He began at the last word, and painted in lively colours the "natural state of man." He showed him lost and hopeless, and with powerful fancy and pathos depicted his certain fate in the defect of any succour. He unquestionably reached the imagination of his hearers with his striking description of the sorrows and penalties of sin; while his analysis of the consciousness of it was singularly complete and startling. Then he showed that Christ Jesus came to save such sinners, and briefly declared the nature and operation of the Atonement. To this succeeded a perfectly irrelevant and gratuitous attack on various other churches!

His exegesis was simple, and his treatment of many points novel and graphic. It was clear that he was more careful to bring these points home to his hearers' hearts than to work out a symmetrical and logical discourse. He concluded with a powerful appeal to them to "accept the Cross," and begin at once a self-dedication to holy life.

Simple as were the elements of the discourse, the effect upon the hearers was very potent. One or two could not restrain their feelings, and had sunk upon their knees sobbing or groaning.

The preacher took advantage of the excitement. He announced that the service would be "protracted" for a while, and in a few words invited those who were "convinced of sin to come up to the communion-rail, where Brothers Patton and Simpson would receive them." Meanwhile the congregation were entreated to pray heartily for the "inquirers." What was the young lord's astonishment to see several persons respond to this invitation, and go forward to kneel in front of the congregation while fervent prayers were offered on their behalf. Every now and then some lively soul in the crowd set up a spontaneous hymn, which was instantly joined in by the people. At the end of half an hour it was announced that "a brother and sister had found peace," and prayers were entreated for others "under conviction." The service was concluded, and the people, in a subdued and solemn manner, prepared to depart, such of them remaining as were entitled to attend the love-feast. Kelso had already obtained permission from one of the "leaders" to be present at this meeting.

VI.—Agape.

To the love-feast persons were admitted by small tokens or tickets. When these had been verified, and one of the brethren had been invited by Dr. Roper to "engage in prayer," baskets containing soft plain biscuits were handed round, followed by large jugs of water, out of which the celebrants drank without the medium of cups. This simple service was performed in silence. The preacher then opened the more serious part of the proceedings with a brief address, which concluded with an intimation that it was free to the brothers or sisters "to give their experience."

"I feel how good the Lord is," said a man, with his eyes shut, and in a trembling voice. "He brought me out of the miry clay; He set my feet upon a rock—He hath established my goings. I served the Devil many years. He tried me sorely. I was the prey of evil passions. I used to gamble, drink, and neglect my work. I was fast going down to Hell. When my Saviour stopped me, I was in the gall of bitterness. One evening as I was going from my work, intending to visit the theatre, a man came up to me in the street, and gave me a tract. He looked at me and said, *The way of transgressors is hard*. I could not get it out of my mind. I felt *my* way was hard. It led me to waste, folly, and ruin. It made every morning a pain with remorse for the deeds of the night before. It made my work unhappy; my amusements were irksome. I read the tract. It was addressed *To the ungodly*. I trembled, I became convinced of sin, I went on my knees and prayed, but could get no comfort. The heavens seemed black above me.

I was in that state for weeks—till one day I happened to be passing a Chapel. I heard singing, and went in—and there I found peace. I have ever since been walking in the way of life. Glory be to God! I am weak, but Christ is strong."

Lord Bantam had listened attentively.

"There is nothing so repulsive in that," whispered Kelso. "Granting the Christian premisses, this man has very simply told a very ordinary experience."

After a long silence, an old woman stood up, and detailed her story in blank verse sentences, with a quavering sing-song, in this wise :—

> I want tu tell ov my luv for Jesus,
> 'Ee luved me an' I luv 'im.
> 'Ee 'av ben a good Säviour tu me :
> 'Ee 'av 'a ben my friend these many 'yers,
> An' shall be ontu death.
> I remembers well 'ow first 'Ee cum tu me.
> I wos young an' silly—fond ov vanity an' shaw—
> O 'ow good of 'im to bear wi' mäy sins !—
> I 'ardened my yeart agenst the 'Oly Wurd.
> My fäather and muther besowt me tu giv
> My yeart to 'im—
>   But I woold not :
> I luved the Oorld, the flesh an' the Devil.
> The day it was 'Ee cum to me—
> —I remembers it clear as yesternday !—
> I went hout in the gloam tu the well for water,
> An' suddenly, jist as I was a unyoalking the päal,
> I saw a bright light drup down upon the well,
> It were like a ball o' fire—an' I yeard 'im säy to me,
> " Meary, why do 'ee 'ate me ? I am yower Saviour."
> —An' I swoonded away !

> When I cum tu I began to pray—
> Thank God I found peace, an' ever since
> I 've served my Saviour.
> Glory be to God.   Aämen.

The old woman subsided amidst a chorus of glories, and Bantam and his tutor took advantage of the break to get away.

*_**

VII.—Human Sympathy in its influence on Catholicity.

THE young lord was for some time lost in thought. So novel and so extraordinary had been the experience of the night, that it seemed to him like a dream—and I am bound to say not a pleasant one. It is a very rude transition from the impassioned dignity and self-control of refined culture or a cool temperament to hysterical emotion and vulgar unrestraint. At length he broke silence.

BANTAM. I hardly know what to think of this. It rakes one's feelings very uncomfortably. Yet I must confess to a strange influence upon me.

KELSO. There would, no doubt, be a certain amount of emotional sympathy amidst such excitement. But try to form a judgment on it.

BANTAM. I am puzzled. I must own we have witnessed earnestness, anxiety, and talent of a peculiar sort in the high business of 'saving souls.' We have also seen apparently genuine feelings of shame, humiliation, anguish, confession, on the part of persons who were unused to such emotions. There must have been people at that communion-rail—as the preacher called it—who two or three hours since had as much intention of going to the moon as of exposing themselves publicly under the influence of acute feeling. How long does this last?

KELSO. With many of them it rapidly passes away, with others it is clearly genuine. It completely alters their lives. Believe me this is so.

BANTAM. But it seems so irrational.

KELSO. But it is a *fact;* and you and I are arguing on the basis of revelation and of a faith in most points common with that of these people. You are discontented more at the *manner* of its action than at the results or the cause of it.

BANTAM. Yes. Their wild emotions, their strange expressions, their crude form of worship, their still more singular exposure of inner feelings and secrets too sacred, I should think, for display to the curiosity of a public meeting, test my charity very much. Are these things consistent with reverence, humility, self-forgetfulness and sincerity?

KELSO. Experience has proved that they are. Many men of as refined a nature as yours have become familiar with these scenes, have themselves passed through such experiences and have afterwards been able to join in them with pleasure. Take Wesley himself for an instance.

Bantam. I could not possibly become accustomed to this sort of thing.

Kelso. Possibly: but it might be owing more to want of sympathy in yourself than to any real defect in the people. This is the religion that suits them—less emotional forms please others—but you must have learned enough to-night to cause you to look with respect and charity even on demonstrations like these. I admit that they contain many objectionable elements.

Bantam. Then there was the old woman! She is a trial to your theory. She repeated that odd and utterly incredible story as if she had learned it off by heart.

Kelso. No doubt she has by constant repetition.

Bantam. But it is untrue.

Kelso. Not quite. Consider her age. What she affects to describe must have happened nearly sixty years ago. I can account for it satisfactorily; so do most of those who hear her. They take it in the figurative sense in which, in her younger days, no doubt, she originally used to couch the recital of her conversion. Gradually the poor old soul, from constant brooding on it, has come to believe that the spiritual influence, which she used to liken to a fire and a voice, did reach her through visible and audible realities, and it does not harm her. She believes in the real thing, which is after all the great matter.

BANTAM. These are phenomena to be studied. I never looked at them in this way before.

KELSO. Very few people do. It needs a large human sympathy to understand the varieties of human feeling and to overlook the mere accidents of its expression. Cultivate that, and you will be astonished to find how many barriers will be broken down between you and your human brothers.

Bantam's method of applying Kelso's principles turned out to be wrong, but to candid men the principles must answer for themselves.

VIII.—Oxbridge.

IT was resolved that the second Lord Bantam should go for a year to the sister university. The inexpediency of sending him to the scene of his brother's errors was obvious. He was therefore entered at the ancient foundation of St. Thomas, in the University of Oxbridge. No one expected him either to work or to win University honours, but it could not be otherwise than a good thing for him to mix in learned society. Up to this time, as we have seen, he had had the advantages of almost hothouse forcing in every branch of learning; of travel; of a precocious introduction to politics; and of intercourse with an extraordinarily vigorous and original mind. As to religion, he had only, I fear, brought away the lesson to be broad without being deep. In fact, admirable and genial as was Kelso's teaching, it could only take root and bear fruit in a groundwork of faith : not the faith of dogmas; not a faith formulated in however perfect a creed ; but a faith *informing*—to use that word in its ancient sense— the life. So different are the outshoots of the same things in different grounds ! Bantam never had a religion—he therefore had none to lose. The charities which his tutor so earnestly enforced upon him, were to him sentiments; they were not living experiences of his soul.

In the University an undergraduate so eminent as our hero in both name and prospects was sure to find free to him the cream of its intellectualism. From the venerable master of his College, from a well-known coterie of mutual admirers in literature and philosophy to obscurer religious or political associations, he was everywhere welcome. A disciple so exalted, such a consociate, was a tower of strength to any theory. The benefit of the strangely diversified intercourse this position afforded him was real enough, but not unalloyed with evil. Opinions in themselves worth little were by the hearers of them weighted with undue gravity when they fell from his lips, and it is not strange that he came to form an extravagant estimate of himself. Moreover the ease with which tolerably clear views of various subjects could be acquired by him in conversation with some of the ablest talkers of the day, tended to divert him from the more thorough and troublesome labour of studying them for himself. Hence by a semi-royal road the child of fortune became an adept without being a student.

His disposition was to philosophic reading and disquisition; and, whether owing most to his hair or the unlucky vaccination or Mr. Kelso's arguments, I cannot say, he soon began to develop "advanced"—even revolutionary tendencies. He affected reading considerably beyond him at that stage of his life—Voltaire, Rousseau, Comte, Bentham, Emerson—and, it proved the wisdom of Agricola's mother as described by Tacitus, that these difficult authors seemed to throw off its balance his too ardent and ambitious mind.

IX.—The Radish Club.

Two clubs of essentially different character at this time existed in Oxbridge. One was the Radish Club, so called from the colour of its opinions and perhaps from their pungency. The Radish Club consisted of what were termed "advanced men." It was said their ideas were revolutionary, but when these came to be examined they were found to be consistent with a great deal of liberalism to existing institutions. True, some of the opinions enunciated by the young gentlemen and two or three professors whose names alone gave any lustre to the club, were startling. Apparently nothing short of an abolition of Queens, Lords, and Commons, and a periodical redistribution of property, would satisfy this blood-red association. At the time, nothing could be less practical or more foolish than such a society. Any one who attentively studied the constitution of England must have seen that with all its faults it was far better adapted to the best purposes of legislative Reform than any other governmental institution in the world. It might in fact be correctly termed a Republican Monarchy, and as, after all, forms of government and political reconstruction are only means to an end, it was well worth considering whether the constitution did not afford every facility for safe and sure social reforms, and whether these were not the matters that at the moment required the gravest attention. But for youths possessed of the "*incensum ac flagrantem animum*,"—as well, alas! as for some statesmen of maturer growth,—the brilliancy of political revolution seems to be more attractive than the humble utilitarian movements of social reform. It is doubtful whether these earnest gentlemen were all so anxious for the success of their opinions as for the sweets of notoriety. Even a tin kettle at the tail may seem to some animals better than absolute oblivion and silence. However, here Bantam was to be persuaded that he himself was an anomaly—a living specimen of unjust laws and unwise political economy; that the monarch was an anachronism; that the purest and best form of government was a republic; that the proper check to the dangers of a republic was education and the minority system of representation; and with this singular programme, and a denial of all religious ideas, this club was prepared to go forth and regenerate or enlighten mankind. In this large project it has hitherto failed, and we have yet to see its influence upon that unit of man, Lord Bantam.

X.—The Essenes.

THE other club was a religious club or rather a club without a religion, since it subjected all faiths to the *à priori* test, and found them wanting; and up to that time had been unable to construct by any eclectic formulæ a system of its own. It was breadth without length or any substance. With that strange straining after paradox that was in vulgar use at the time, the members called themselves The Essenes, although in fact they combined the self-conceit of the Pharisees with the scepticism of the Sadducees. The meetings of this club, which were held on Sunday evenings, took place in the rooms of a fellow and tutor of some eminence, whose father, the Rev. Shadrach Ventom, had been a famous dissenting minister. His son, Reginald Ventom, distinguishing himself at a grammar school, won a mathematical scholarship, and with a robust body and unwearied industry attained the position of Senior Wrangler. Of no particular religious bias, he had not permitted his father's creed to interfere with his own elevation, and had qualified for a fellowship by making a declaration that was untrue—an event too common to be worth criticising in this instance. With equal indifference, and for the same purpose, he adopted the clerical profession. Let any one read carefully the Service for the Ordination of Deacons in the Book of Common Prayer, if he would gauge the unconscientious nature of this proceeding and the deadness of a moral sense which could face that solemn ordeal with indifference, much more with disdain. I cannot say it affected his belief. He had never been troubled with any. His mind was large—his body healthy—his instincts were animal—he was wide in his sympathies, though these to a shrewd observer seemed rather assumed and sensational—easy-going rather than principled in his charity. He thought he was always looking for truth, but in fact he was never expecting to find it. From the narrowness of his father's creed he had turned with abhorrence. It was far too exacting, too inspired with the idea of sacrifice, for a man unprepared to concede to any religion more than a fraction of his being. He sought for, and was content with, a

THE ESSENES.

general average of good in mankind; that is, in all portions not "Evangelical." Towards that section, whom he called "Calvinists," he ceased to be charitable, he was vindictive.

Round him Ventom had attracted a coterie of similarly easy-fitting minds. These gentlemen made the loudest professions of catholicity. They took an ostentatious interest in lower-class propagandism. Their humanity was extravagant. Their sentimental protests against evil and wrong were even exaggerated. Their breadth was enormous. They professed to find in Quakerism symptoms of "a philosophic basis of practical religion;" viewed in Methodism, "some aspects of the highest evidences of an emotional spiritualism;" and studied Mormonism in its phenomena of "an abnormal development of the divine ideas." In their researches among these "peculiar phases of fetishism" they also included investigations into the unnatural outbreaks of human enthusiasm, whereof a work of some notoriety, entitled "Hyper-Transcendent Spouses," was a fitting text-book. They were Athenian in their readiness to hear every new thing—but their credulity was reserved for negatives. Compare all this with the lesson which Kelso had drawn for the young Lord from their singular visits to various sectarian services.

It is impossible to deny the charm wherewith this breadth of theoretic sympathy enveloped the society. It seemed as if the millennium had dawned in a few preliminary streaks upon a dozen or two of commonplace students in that unlikely place. No man's faith was actually despised—nor was any man's unbelief matter of abhorrence. They professed to be scientific searchers after truth, and regarded the religions as part of their facts. *A priori* was their watchword against an antiquated authoritative formula, *Thus saith the Lord*. If it was an advantage of their religious art that it had no principle, it was a natural correlative that it had no practice.

Between these two associations Lord Bantam's principles and politics assumed an alarming shape. He began to astonish his tutors by his political contortions and the breadth of his disbelief; but throwing over faith is not throwing over credulity. In fact he became a conspicuous instance of that increasingly common paradox, a credulous believer in anything that is unbelief. This was very far beyond Mr. Kelso, and doubtless a partial reason of his extravagance was, that he had heard Mr. Kelso's conclusions, without reaching the bases of that vast fabric of knowledge on which they were built. The change was gradual. He at first professed to be a Catholic in the broadest sense—to recognise the good in all, the pre-eminence of none. Then he disclaimed the superiority of the Bible over other philosophical or religious authorities, and shifted the tests from the field of revelation to that of *à priori* reasoning. This is dangerous, unless a man has an almost infinite range of knowledge, for *à priori* to ignorant or half-instructed minds is little else than *Ego*.

The bonds of religion and the restraints of society became equal wrongs in his eyes. He saw in property a robbery of the community by a selfish individual. He saw in church and dogma a tyranny over the individual by the community. These anomalies it would be his duty to help to redress. He was clearly unfitting himself for the respectable superstition and the selfish complacency necessary to sustain the rôle of an aristocrat.

PART IV.

HOW HE CAME TO YEARS OF DISCRETION AND OTHERWISE.

I.—Citizen Bantam.

LORD BANTAM returned home from the University. He might now claim to be somewhat of a man. His title had brought him in contact with men who without it would scarcely have condescended to talk with him. The care taken with his education had produced some fruit in qualifying him to take a prominent position at the Union. His reputation as a fluent speaker had transcended the bounds of the university. He was shortly to come of age. The Earl and Countess had been considering plans for those vast festivities which were, in accordance with aristocratic custom, to signalise this event. The stewards of the various estates, manors, mines and properties, had been invited to send suggestions for the proper celebration, in their respective jurisdictions, of the heir's majority; and the Earl's chamberlain was over head and ears in plans, estimates and contracts connected with the approaching fêtes. The Countess referred to the trouble one day in a jocose manner to her son who, having taken earnestly to the study of the French philosophy, paid little attention to family matters.

"You must really throw away your books for awhile," said she, "and help us in devising how to bring you out with due honour. It's an affair of months, for you know we have thousands of people to provide for."

"To provide for thousands of people! What for?"

"For the fêtes on your coming of age. The heir to the wealthiest earldom in England must have no ordinary rejoicings on attaining his majority."

"Rejoicings! My dear mother, what is a birthday? And what is the good of rejoicing because I have attained a certain anniversary? You would put me on a par with young Foley, who is the greatest idiot I know; and they say his people spent ten thousand pounds to celebrate his reaching the indifferent age of twenty-one years. Surely, my father," he added, with a twinkle of satire, "won't waste any money on my majority."

"Indeed, he will," replied her ladyship, "and more than ten thousand if it is necessary. On a matter of that kind no one shall surpass us."

"Well, then, my dear mother, let me tell you what to do with the money. Give it away, and spare the folly and licence and absurdity of such an exhibition in a civilised country."

"Folly, Albert! Licence! Absurdity! in a civilised country. What *do* you mean?"

"I mean that I am ashamed of my position, one I have done nothing to deserve, and one quite inconsistent with social rights. Altogether, I am pained that I should succeed to so much while others succeed to nothing; and my claim to a title ought not to depend on my being born to it, but should be proved by my work. I am entirely opposed to an aristocracy at all, and only wish I had been born in a garret. Instead of spending money on fêtes we should be ashamed to celebrate our own monstrous selfishness."

"Good God!" said the Countess, "what has befallen you? How wildly you are talking. Why, sir, you don't deserve your good fortune. Born in a garret forsooth! Oh, I see," added the poor Countess, covering her eyes as his red hair flashed upon them, but too good a woman and too noble a lady to allude to *that* to her son, "that horrid vaccination! I knew it would be so!"

"Vaccination, Lady Ffowlsmere; what can that have to do with my opinions?"

"You were vaccinated from that Radical child, and I am sure it has affected you," said the Countess, having recourse to her handkerchief.

Bantam heard of his Radical vaccination for the first time, and was highly amused, not to say gratified to learn that he had some vulgar fluid in his body. He strove to comfort his mother, while he smiled at her superstition, at the same time assuring her that he could not conscientiously allow himself to be made the subject of any foolish demonstrations. He preferred to be considered "Citizen Bantam;" and to give away a few thousands in charity would please him better than any number of feasts and rejoicings. I need not say that every word he spoke was making the Countess worse. His vaccination had "taken" with a vengeance.

II.—A Rank Communist.

THE Countess said not a word to the Earl about her curious conversation with our hero. The preparations went on. She wisely resolved to allow her husband to find out his son's views for himself. The *dénouement* was not long in coming.

One morning the trio were seated at the breakfast table in Hiton Place, her ladyship sipping her coffee, the young lord deep in the leaders of the *Chimes*, and the Earl reading his letters, when an unusually angry exclamation from the peer startled his companions.

BANTAM. What's the matter, my lord?

EARL. That stupid fellow Cringeley, steward of my Penshurst property, has failed in an action of ejectment; it will cost me a pretty penny. He wrote me, he was certain of succeeding as he had retained all the best counsel on the Circuit. Now he tells me that the tenant specially retained that clever fellow Hawkeye, the sharpest advocate in England, and they've succeeded—not even a point of law reserved by the Chief Justice.

BANTAM. What was the point?

EARL. The tenant Turfman has a long lease at a low rental, and has been at sword's-point with my people down there for the last five years. They have been keeping a sharp look-out on him, in the hope of finding a chance to turn him out—he's rather a speculative needy sort of fellow, I think : actually stood for Parliament once —a tenant farmer—stood for the House, and was beaten two to one, and serve him right. His property lies very awkwardly right across the estate, and somehow or other he tricked old Ball, Cringeley's predecessor, into giving him a lease with right to destroy all the ground game. Since then rabbits have become very valuable, and if it were not for that restraint on the game, the whole of which he prevents from crossing the estate, we could make £200 a year out of that alone. But this infernal fellow comes between. He keeps terriers, and not a single lop-ear dare show itself his side of the hedge.

BANTAM. But you don't mean to say, my lord, you object to that? Ground game destroy cultivation. It's contrary to good management to encourage it at all. I wouldn't have a lop-ear on my estate. And the man has his rights has he not? Is it a question of money?

EARL. Why, sir, of course it is; I'm entitled to make all I can out of my property.

BANTAM. Yes, subject to his rights legal and moral, and your duties legal and moral, my lord; and I may also add, the proper economy of society.

EARL. I am aware of that, Lord Bantam, except as to what you call "the proper economy of society," which I take to be that every man must look out for himself; but I may be allowed to regret, that owing to the folly of my former agent I am proscribed from controlling my own estate: and owing to the incapacity of the present one I have not recovered that power.

BANTAM. But, my dear father, do you mean to say that you have put this poor fellow to the expense of defending his tenancy, because your agent thought he had detected some flaw in his conduct which worked a forfeiture of his lease?

EARL. Good heavens! sir, why not?

BANTAM. Why, my lord, because it is inhuman and unjust for you, a great Earl, with an immense income, to take advantage of any such circumstances to injure, perhaps to ruin a man who happens to be inconvenient to you. Admitting you were legally right it seems to me that agent of yours has acted most iniquitously, and you ought to pay the poor man's expenses. If not, you will have used your superior wealth and position to damage the rights of a man entitled to perfect equality with yourself before God and the country.

EARL. Heyday, my young moralist, what have "God and the country" to do with my property at Penshurst, I wonder? And hasn't the man an equality as you call it? He goes before a jury, and gets his rights just as I do.

BANTAM. No, he has not an equality. He seems to have; that is to say the law treats him exactly as it treats you, but you have the advantage. You can afford to be indifferent to the result, he cannot. Cringeley with your money bought up all the available talent of the Circuit to help to win your case—which if it were an honest one ought not to need it—in the hope of gaining an unfair advantage. That is legal, but is it fair dealing between man and man? He was luckily able to checkmate you, by getting a first-class advocate; but I suppose at great expense, perhaps a ruinous one. He has not been treated generously, or as one fellow-citizen ought to be treated by another; therefore I take it he is wronged. This is not social communism or equality of rights.

The Earl was accustomed to command his temper, or he might have received this harangue with a resentment fatal to the forward young gentleman's political education. He gave a long low whistle.

EARL. What do you think of that, Lady Ffowlsmere? *Social Communism! Equality of Rights!* is that what you have learnt at Oxbridge? However (said the old diplomatist, smiling), you may thank your stars, sir, that your condition and prospects will compel you to drop these dangerous heresies. A man with half a million a year is not likely to be a Communist.

The young lord stoutly maintained, amid deprecating cries from his mother, that he was a Communist and in favour of an equal distribution of property. The Earl became amused. The joke was too good. For the wealthiest man in England to advocate Communism, was like a bishop preaching the untruthfulness of Moses. So he terminated the discussion by retreating to his library, where for a long time he might have been heard whistling,

> In Holland there dwelt a Mynheer Von Clam
> Who every morning said, 'I am
> The richest merchant in Rotterdam.'

—" and," said he to himself, "a Communist! He! He! He!"

* *

III.—A School for Fledgling Nobles.

LORD FFOWLSMERE was a shrewd, long-headed man. He maintained towards his son the most perfect kindliness. His policy, declared to and approved by the Countess, was to offer no opposition to the young lord's whims. He even compromised the majority matter. There was to be but one celebration, at Shufflestraw Castle, to which all his Shufflestraw tenants and the inhabitants generally of the town of Ffowlsmere were to be invited. For the rest, the day was to be signalised by concessions to the tenants on the various estates, and by the distribution of gifts to vast numbers of *employés*. Moreover, sundry charities were to be some thousands the better of the heir's majority.

The distressing peculiarities of the youth led the Earl to consider that it would be healthy to divert his attention as soon as possible from theoretic and philosophic to practical politics. In working out these, he conceived, his son's ideas would gradually be led to harmonize more completely with the spirit of the age and the principles proper to his station. He took an opportunity of broaching this to Lord Bantam, suggesting that soon after he was qualified he should prepare himself to take a seat in the House of Commons. Valuable institution, which affords a free school of politics to an unoccupied aristocracy!

"Every young man in your position should obtain a seat in the Lower House first. It brings him in contact with the most powerful body in the kingdom, and with men who are the best tutors in political principles and tactics. It also enables him to judge of the tendency of present legislation, and is a training-school for office, should he have the ability to obtain it. The actual power of the House of Peers as a House is decreasing, but that decrease of power may be partially balanced by taking every opportunity to acquire, through relatives or nominees, increased representation in the Lower Chamber. As leader of the party in the Upper House, I shall no doubt be able to seat you. I have several places of my own, but I think you should aim at some popular constituency, where your return would be a triumph to you, and an actual gain of influence to me. I can always get safe men for my boroughs."

"I am sure, my lord," said the incorrigible Bantam, "you are sincerely anxious for my welfare; but I am very sorry that neither my opinions nor my ambition coincide with yours. A man should go into Parliament with a purpose, with some inspiration of a duty to be done; not as the tool of his party, or even of his own ambition——"

"Oh! hang your opinions," says the Earl. "I'll take the risk of that. I want you to learn politics—"

"But how can I possibly work with you, my dear father? I am a Radical, you are a Prig. I wish to see all undue influences in the State neutralized; you wish to strengthen them. You desire to give the people exactly the least freedom that will pacify them. I wish to see complete and unqualified acknowledgment of their just rights. I cannot help deeming myself the most unfortunate man in the world! There is no scope for my ambition. I am placed on an aristocratic tramway; I must either run along it, or run off to ruin and confusion."

"Most fortunate for you, sir, that you are so restricted. Many would be glad to change places with you. You are the most unreasonable man I ever heard of! You are unworthy of your good fortune."

"Good fortune, my lord! The best fortune is a good conscience and a true high aim in the world. And what are my hopes? Those of every young peer who keeps himself respectable. I may enter the House of Commons for a few years, and there by judicious airing of my democratic sympathies startle the middle-class men into raptures. I may even manage to absorb into my nature by a sort of endosmose——"

"Hem!" said the Earl.

—"Some notion of the feelings and aspirations of the lower classes, and be enthusiastic awhile against my own. But should you decease—which God avert in my lifetime!—custom decrees that I should cast away my private opinions and accept an uncongenial rôle. In the House of Lords I could not be a democrat. The air would freeze my enthusiasm. Vainly should I ply my lance against the hide of class prejudice! I should become a bore, a nuisance, a malapert, a madman; not only inside, but worst of all, outside the House. No other arena would be open to my ardent desire for propagandism, but that of which the stump is the rostrum; and I fear if I tried it the people would soon tumble me off that as an asinine incongruity. Even the most extreme of them would never believe a peer, who practically disendowed and disestablished himself, to be a man of sense."

"Hum!" said the Earl; who had noticed with some inward satisfaction, how precociously the young man expressed and argued his views, the more since at the same time he recognised the barriers that shut him in from any other destiny.

* *
*

IV.—A Proletarian Compliment.

THE festivities which marked Lord Bantam's attainment of manhood require no lengthened notice from the historian. In one respect they were remarkable, and I select that particular as a subject of history.

Shufflestraw Castle, through its broad sweep of lawn and park, its beechen walks, its terraces and courts, and even over its cold grey stones and battlemented towers, wore the brilliant tokens of a festal time. Flags and banners, tents and pavilions, triumphal arches and vast wreaths or festoons of leaves and flowers everywhere entertained the eye; while under and among them all thousands of brightly-dressed and happy-faced people enlivened the scene. The sounds of trumpets or bands, the ringing shouts, the voices of some impromptu choir cheered the soft sleepy air of a summer's day. Over the park, under the broad-timbered, ancient beeches, far away by the glittering lake, and in and through the sloping tents thronged the tenants of the estate and the middle and lower classes of Ffowlsmere. In the castle-rooms or its trim gardens, over its brilliantly flowered terraces, among the gay pavilions circled the aristocracy of the county and the vast concourse of the Earl's relations. Staid elders chatted softly in gilded summer-houses; happy couples loitered in the pleached walks, or sat on the soft turf, listening to the plash and bubble of the fountains; youths and misses crowded the canvas theatre, wherein the prima donnas of the day gave the tribute of their sweet voices to a young noble's birth—for a consideration. You would have said that all went merry as a marriage-bell.

But in the midst of this happiness there were two disturbing elements. One was the heir himself. He looked or affected to look with disgust upon the huge outcry made about so simple an occurrence as the anniversary of his birth. The other was nothing less than the obnoxious Broadbent, now an old man of rugged and leonine aspect, the Nestor of the Socialists of Ffowlsmere, the person whose blood had tainted the body of Bantam with revolutionary matter. What was he doing at Shufflestraw Castle?

When notice was given to the Mayor and Council of Ffowlesmere that the noble Earl and Countess requested the honour of the company of the aforesaid dignitaries of the town and the rest of its inhabitants at the festivities to take place on the attainment of the majority of Lord Bantam; and when they, in accordance with instructions to that effect, forwarded to every house a gilded and emblazoned card conveying this invitation and calling upon all good and loyal inhabitants to come forward and represent the town in a proper and becoming manner; and when they proposed that an address to the Earl and his Lady and to the young Lord, should be drawn up "for the auspicious occasion," and engrossed upon vellum in notable and brilliant characters, Broadbent's brows met in a portentous frown. Here was nobility patronising the sovereign people. Not only that, it was trying to bribe them to acquiesce in their own enslavement in the old way, through "guzzling and soddening, getting at their hearts by way of their bellies," said Mr. B. And here were the guardians of the freedom of a free town proposing to "kotow to a *blank* Fetish." Mr. Broadbent determined all this should not pass unchallenged. He was a shoemaker, a man we have said of leonine countenance, grizzly, big-browed. Why is it that shoemakers are so often revolutionary? Is it that their cramped attitude, notwithstanding the hard muscular employment of their arms, induces indigestion and morbidity? Mr. Broadbent was a good talker, a strong thinker, well-read and astute. He concocted a remonstrance against the proposed address in terms the reverse of parliamentary, and sent it round to his compact little party for signature. The town council considered it for three hours with closed doors, and eventually resolving "not to consider it, on account of its improper terms," returned it to the memorialists. Upon this Broadbent changed his tactics. He and his friends accepted the invitations to the castle; and here they were all together, lying and talking apart from the general throng under a clump of trees in the park. It was clear they had something in hand. So the mayor and council thought, and so they suggested to the Earl's steward. Consequently, some of those gentlemen denominated " policemen in plain clothes" were always loitering in the neighbourhood of this dangerous body.

The day wore on, and tables, groaning under noble loads, were rapidly released from the incubus, and oceans of jolly ale or finer tipples told not only on the feelings but on the spirits of the guests. At length a great bell rang out a signal for a general concourse, and preceded by a fine band a procession in which Lord Bantam occupied an honourable though awkward place, filing majestically out of the castle, wended its way to a gloriously decorated platform, in front of which on the green turf thousand of seats had been prepared. Then addresses from tenants and others were delivered, and a general toast was drunk, and universal enthusiasm was culminating towards the point of the young lord's speech, when the aforesaid leonine head of Broadbent—an apparition at which the Countess shuddered and hid her face—was raised upon four strong shoulders, and he, holding up a scroll in his hand, in a steady voice asked leave to present the young lord with another address. At the same moment a few rough-looking Titans closed round the old man, while through the crowd as by one impulse twenty or thirty determined men evidently bent on dissolving the shoemaker's party were seen converging on the spot. The clever old Earl took the cue in a moment. Holding up his hand for silence he called out :—

"I think I recognise Mr. Broadbent, an old friend." Mr. Broadbent's grimace was a study. "I see he wishes to present some memorial. I am sorry we did not know of it before so as to have arranged for its reception; but if you will kindly open the way for Mr. Broadbent and his friends, we will make room for them on the platform."

In a few minutes, dukes, marquises, earls, and their correlatives in the female department had vacated twenty chairs in the very front and midst of that brilliant throng, and thither with the deepest gravity and attention the republicans were escorted by two stewards. They came up the back steps boldly enough, but when they stood out in face of the noble assemblage, and felt themselves riddled with the quiet, cynical stare of hundreds of eyes, they looked rather abashed. Even their leader was afflicted with awkwardness. But he recovered himself, like a wild beast at bay.

"Earl Fiowlsmere," he said, "I and my friends are here to-day by your invitation, but not of our own liking. We are simple townsmen asking only our rights, and wishing to interfere with no one else's. You invited us; we did not want to see your heir or to mix with your aristocratic friends "—looking round on the imperturbable array about him, their quiet *hauteur* stung him—"Some of them, perhaps," added he, "not the folk for honest people to mix with."

There was a roar from the front and the broad shoulders of hundreds of men rose uneasily from the seats among the crowd. Broadbent saw that he had only done a vulgar thing and made some foolish sort of apology, which was received as imperturbably as the insult. A beckon from the Earl sent all the broad shoulders down beside wives and sweethearts again, and from that moment the whole assembly entered into the spirit of his treatment of this insolent intrusion.

Just at this moment, Lord Bantam stepped forward and held out his hand to Broadbent, who after a little hesitation shook it heartily. Then Broadbent went on:

"Those who think with me—no offence meant—think that the day of aristocracy has gone by. We think it is a monstrous injustice that vast estates like this, with all these broad lands, pretty as they are, should be kept for the amusement of a few select persons and not adapted for the benefit of all. You Earl Ffowlsmere never did anything to entitle you to your enormous wealth, never worked for it, and do little good with it; and your son is the same. He takes it from you in the same way, and he will use or abuse it just as you do. And to-day you are celebrating the preliminary of that injustice, and I say your feast is taken from the poor man's table, and your joy is robbed from the poor man's comfort, and your pleasure is bought with the poor man's blood." Another great roar from the crowd. Then Lord Bantam said:

"I think, Mr. Broadbent, you have an address to present; I shall be happy to receive it."

"Oh, you want to stop my mouth, young man? Well, it's no use talking, perhaps. By your leave I'll read you a short address."

The old man placed his wide-awake on the platform, put the scroll of paper between his bandy legs, took out a large wooden spectacle case from his pocket, and withdrew therefrom a mammoth pair of pebbles rimmed with a broad brass frame; these being duly adjusted, the sun slanting across his big shock head and lighting up the grizzly hairs, he looked so like an ancient owl that a roar of laughter enlivened the whole audience from platform to turf. The address was plainly constructed on an American model.

"To Citizen Albert Alfred Augustus Adolphus Loftus Cicely Chester Bantam, the protest and remonstrance of the undersigned people of England:

"*Whereas* Poverty is abroad in her cruellest and most shocking forms; and

"*Whereas* the feudal system and all that springs from it is the bane and curse of this country.

"*Whereas* aristocracy is an absurd and unjust privilege conferred on the least worthy and most indolent portion of society.

"*Whereas* it has been declared on high authority that if a man will not work neither shall he eat.

"*Whereas* the locking up of vast domains of land in the hands of a few persons is socially and politically and economically and morally" [as the old man rolled out these portentous words shouts of laughter rent the air] "unjust.

"*Whereas* the only true principles of government are Liberty, Equality, and Fraternity, and no right ought to be recognised not common to all.

"*Whereas* it is expedient at once to begin to establish the Great, True, and Universal Republic, to abolish all titles, and to legislate for the equalisation of property :

"We, the undersigned, as brother citizens, address you on the occasion of your attaining to an age of discretion, the age when you are permitted to exercise your civil rights.

"We hail you as a brother citizen entitled to the same privileges with ourselves and nothing more.

"We protest against your assumption of a title unearned by any great or noble acts of yours ; and ask you as a brother and a citizen to repudiate it.

"We protest further against your succession to the unrighteously excessive amount of property which the law has impolitically permitted your forefathers to accumulate.

"Wherefore we pray that you will consider the rights of the poor, who are your fellow men, and will pledge yourself that you will, on attaining to the inordinate property of which you are the heir, distribute it among your brother citizens——"

Roars of laughter drowned the remainder of the sentence and the names of the memorialists. Then Broadbent, handing the scroll to the young lord, took off his spectacles and donned his chapeau. He was accommodated with a seat. Meanwhile Lord Bantam, taking off his hat, stood forward, the sun flaunting brilliantly on his auricomous poll. The cheery cheering, the waving hats and kerchiefs, the tears that stood in old and young folks' eyes were enough to soften any man.

"My lords, ladies and gentlemen, and *brother citizens*"—turning to the republicans—"I know not in what terms to express the emotion which your affectionate and cordial greetings stir in my heart. I have never so thoroughly felt the privilege of manhood, of human sympathy (cheers). I thank you every one, from my dear father and mother who take so deep an interest in my happiness, and whose best gift to me in life has been the example of noble conduct (great cheering), and the advantages of training under their eye; from these, I say, my nearest and dearest, through the long list of my other relatives, to you all, whoever and whatever you may be. Specially let me say do. I thank my brother citizens (laughter and cheers) who have come here to-day to remind me of that which I have not forgotten, which to confess to you all the real truth is a burthen on my heart this day—of an inequality of conditions resulting from impolitic laws and upheld on unjust principles."

If you know what it is to see something like a chill shudder pass through a vast assemblage, you may picture to yourself the effect of these words on Lord Bantam's amazed hearers. The Earl was biting his lip viciously and repeating his Rotterdam formula to himself in a sort of desperation; the brother and sister aristocracy were amused, the bucolic crowd was dazed or thunderstruck.

"Yes, my friends, I believe, and would have you all believe, that much which is contained in this scroll is true, and needs to be thought on sacredly and seriously by those who in such a position as I to-day occupy are the invidious claimants of extravagant rights (No, no). I say Yes! yes! and I cannot as a conscientious man but have much sympathy with the position taken by Mr. Broadbent and his friends."

At this point Bantam's eye happened to light on his mother who was weeping hysterically. Simultaneously a lusty voice far down in the middle remarked,

"E doänt moind that d—d Broädbent, do'ee? E aint yer brother no more than Oi be!"

An inadequate joke which made a perfect earthquake

in the human mass. Bantam's heart smote him, and the resolution which he had long been forming to discharge this day, with heroic courage, the duty of repudiating all aristocratic theories, rights and appointments, succumbed to his affection. With a few more words he sat down.

Is it not possible for a man to make an abjectly heroical fool of himself? It would be painful to describe the morphitic change that came over the spirit of the festivities, except among the Republicans, and their triumph was so dubious that the Earl wisely provided them a picked escort to their homes. The aristocrats simply wondered. Most of them seemed to think it was the privilege of an heir to be wilful, and were inclined to take it as a joke. A few who were in the secret exchanged significant whispers respecting the dangers of republican vaccination.

V.—Newspaper Moralisers.

OUR hero's singular escapade was sure not to escape the notice of the press. In fact it was reported at large in the county papers and formed the theme of not a few articles in those of the metropolis. The young lord's character, and the effect of his declarations on his father's political influence, were discussed with remarkable frankness. The *Banner* put him down as "one of those priggish young gentlemen whom the new educational influences at work in Oxbridge University were sending broadcast into the world with the shallowest hold on religion, morals, true political principles or common sense."

But it was the *Chimes* which rang out with the most solemn grandeur on this event. It was peculiarly a case for them. They could not refrain from preaching a sermon to the unwise and inexperienced youth who had so early, so publicly and at so inopportune a time declared himself for principles incompatible with the common sense of mankind. "Lord Bantam," it said, "has proved himself even younger than his age. He appears not to have imbibed from his tutors at Oxbridge the very elementary principles of economy—principles no man can either subvert or disdain. The ideal theorizing which leads men to the absurd conclusions of equality is only dangerous because it makes its appeal at once to the basest passions and the most stupid ignorance. The doctrine of the Commune lies at the base of the ideas—propagated shall we say?—nay, that have miscarried in Lord Bantam's brain. A perfect junior in his own class, he has foolishly gone out of his way to attack it. He has not yet apprehended the high privileges of his birth. He proves incapable of considering its relations to the social system. Nor has he examined by how nice an adjustment of our social structure and our legislative action, we have gradually reached a state close upon political perfection. In the fact that he will succeed to the name and the estates of his father, irrespectively of any simple accidents of ability or industry, he should have discerned a reason recognised by the wisdom of our forefathers. The fact that without our aristocracy our system of government would not be what it is, exposes at once the amazing shallowness of the ideas embraced and avowed by the heir of one of the wealthiest and noblest of our great houses," &c. &c. To find in the existence of a thing a reason for its existence is a form of fallacious reasoning not uncommon with some of the leaders of public opinion.

***

VI.—Economic Notes.

THE Earl, whatever his chagrin at the exhibition so infelicitously made by his son, showed no sign of it to the latter, and before the world treated it with that dry good-humoured deprecation which disarms the bitterest critic. He sagely conceived the idea of permitting the young man to see the extent of his prospective wealth. Accordingly, as the shooting season was nigh, he arranged that they should make a tour of all the estates, finishing the magnificent progress in Scotland, at the half royal seat of Drumdrum Castle, whither he invited a select and numerous company.

Lord Bantam acquiesced with alacrity in a proposal

which promised him a rare opportunity of studying the social questions just then exercising his mind. He had paid several surreptitious visits to the notorious Broadbent, who somewhat further enlightened him upon the views entertained by the proletariat on the land question. He began to feel an uneasy sense of injustice in his position present and prospective. One object that he set before him as a motive to his journey, was to ascertain the number and classes of persons then gaining a livelihood on the Earl's domains, and to institute a comparison between that and the possible results of a dissipation of his property through the community; as to the latter branch, clearly a vague, impracticable inquiry for him; with regard to which endless theorizing, innumerable arguments from analogy and multitudinous examples or illustrations from other states of society would obviously be necessary if any useful demonstration were to come out of his labours.

I ought not to attempt to follow him over the entire field of his inquiries. I subjoin, however, an abbreviated copy of a schedule drawn up by him, with some more extended notes upon one of the Metropolitan estates, that of Crane Gardens.

There was a root of wisdom in the young lord's proceeding, not yet so far as I know properly unearthed by busy reforming economists. To apply their industry in ascertaining and comparing the respective numbers of persons that *do* make a living out of a huge estate, and the maximum that *might* be maintained on and out of it; and from the results to invent some system which, without wrong to any living person or perilous disregard of economic laws, should tend to encourage the distribution of the land among the aforesaid maximum, is the problem of problems for us to solve in England just now. Look not at it askance, O ye select and Heaven-ordained body of Primogenials—*it* must be solved or *you* be dissolved. It is a question between you and the Maximum! To it honest Reformers! Not with malicious animosity against a peerage, though possibly you may find that to be inextricably involved in the land system, or with insensate envy of wealth, or with mere revolutionary passion, but in the pure, healthy, earnest impulse of a deliberate reform spirit. The land must no longer be for the few but for the many. Pray and work that the transfer may be made without confiscation or plunder or terror through a gradual process of solvent legislation!

NOTES BY LORD BANTAM.

"*Coal Mines in Blackshire.* I found that upon the Collieries there were employed the following persons :—A manager, £2,000 per annum, and 1 per cent. on returns; steward, 2½ per cent. on profits, per annum; 4 overmen, £250 per annum each; an engineer, £400 per annum; 2 assistant ditto, at £250 per annum each; consulting engineer, £300 per annum; 16 viewers, £2,400; engine-drivers, stokers, fitters, boiler-makers, carpenters, £1,350; platelayers, blacksmiths, etc., £720; stablemen and horses, £2,100; colliers, butties, putters, etc., etc., 3,850 men and boys, £180,200 per annum. Total, £192,870. Office book-keepers and clerks, £1,400 per annum. I found also that the solicitors for this property, whose main work I should judge was taking care of the title deeds, generally contrived to bring up their bill to £3,000 per annum. The steward receives £4,507 10s., and the manager, additional, £3,750; making the expense £205,127 10s., out of an annual return of £375,000.

On this I note that probably these mines can be most efficiently worked by a great capitalist, and could not well be subdivided into small proprietorships; but, on the other hand, when I looked at the labourers, and saw how terrible was the work they had to do, and how little real interest they had in its results; when I saw how much went into the coffers of one who hardly ever saw them, and perhaps rarely thought of their existence except as useful machines for the creation of income; when I saw how much agents and parasites were making out of this property compared with those to whose labour it owed its value; when I saw, above all, the hovels in which they herded together—small, foul, pestilential, and found that the Manager, in his endeavour to economise, had even failed to provide them in their mines with the ventilating shafts necessary for safety and health, or those facilities of exit from their dreadful labour, which with any other brutes would be deemed indispensable; when I found on inquiry that many of the little boys I saw employed in these places were no older than ten, and worked as many hours a day, without education, with nothing that could be called recreation, with no variety save the regular transition from the *inferno* below to purgatory above; I had a sickening sense that the system under which all this exists was inhuman—the society which permits it rotten —the man who grows rich by it criminal. My father's profits are £170,872 per annum! It cannot long endure. Surely property has other duties than the mere payment of wages and reception of profits! And, as it seems to me, under the best economic regulations, there would be some coöperation between capitalist and workman by which the latter—contributing his due share to the adventure—might be elevated from a state akin to brutality to self-respect and independence. It cannot be called economy to suffer that most valuable article, a man, to go to waste, or to waste himself, if anything can be done to prevent it.

It will be seen at once by any economist, that the young man's generosity and inexperience affected his judgment. Such sentiments as these belong, according to the best authorities, to the unreal dreams of the Commune, not to the sober resolutions of Manchester finance.

Here is another leaf from Lord Bantam's note-book.

"*METROPOLITAN PROPERTY.*
"*THE CRANE GARDENS ESTATE.*

"Consisting of 5 squares: 22 streets: mews, gardens, &c., &c. Include 2,125 houses, the ground, held by 54 tenants under the head leases at 99 years: their holdings varying from £200 to £3,000 a year. Total income per annum £55,700

"*Mem.* It may be taken that there are 2,125 tenants of as many houses. These houses are of a good class, and may be taken to average in value at least £200 a year, which is of course paid to the 54 lessees or their assigns, &c., by the sub-tenants.

"To collect the Earl's rents and attend generally to the legal business arising out of his interest in his estate, one firm of solicitors is employed, who manage to return to my father's chamberlain a bill for between £2,000 and £3,000 a year. Two collectors of rents are also employed at a salary of £200 a year.

"Few law suits, and no defaults, since the land is now worth many times the head rents.

"No rates or taxes on the ground landlord, except income tax.

"*Mem.* The Earl therefore pockets the whole of this large revenue out of this parish without making any contribution to its rates, and might live and spend his money out of the kingdom with equal immunity from the local burdens. *Qy.* Justice of this?

"*Note.* The property represented by this great income is immovable. Practically it never changes hands, it is not divisible, it does not come into the market. The only dealing is in the subordinate leaseholds; clearly a very different thing from sale and exchange of freeholds. The persons to whom that part of the property which is represented by this income of £55,700 a year gives employment are few, and they are mere parasites. But suppose there had been a separate owner for say every under-tenancy—had 2,125 freeholders been living and dying, marrying and making settlements, becoming bankrupt, mortgaging, selling, buying, the amount of healthy action in this commodity, land, would have been enhanced many fold more than it can possibly be at present. *N.B.* The permutations and combinations to be considered. *Also*, to take into consideration probable number of dealings in the limited and more restricted interests, created by the relations of landlords and tenants; both as under existing régime, and under the hypothetical division of the freehold amongst many holders."

Another memorandum made by Lord Bantam at the time, noted on a loose digressive sheet, marked *Private*, deserves to be transcribed. He says, in his dry way:

"Among the uses of an aristocracy, with its wealth so elaborately and carefully pillared up by the joint ingenuity of class-selfishness and the laws—one would deem not the least important to be, that it should take the lead in all schemes of rational benevolence or social improvement, imparting body and vigour to charity—and proving how beneficial to society these anomalous aggregations of resources in one hand can be made.

"Knowing that my father was a fair specimen of aristocratic benevolence, I took some pains to ascertain, wherever I went, what local or general charities received his assistance. I take it that his average income is £700,000 a year.

"Last year out of this sum, so far as I can learn, he made the following donations. I remember seeing some of them described in the newspapers as 'munificent.'

"To build a 'Ffowlsmere wing' to the 'Royal Hospital for Unendurables' £5,000
To the 'Crane Gardens' Hospital,' 'Bellowsbury Hospital,' 'Artisan's Institution at Ffowlsmere,' 'Restoration of Duncansby Abbey,' 'Idiots' Asylum,' 'Blackshire distress,' etc., etc., ten donations of £1,000 each 10,000
Fifteen Subscriptions at £500 each 7,500
Twenty „ „ £100 each 2,000
Sundries 1,225

Total . . . £25,725

Say about $\frac{1}{28}$ of an income perfectly safe, liable to few fluctuations except that of increase, and on which he pays comparatively lighter taxes than burden several millions of his compatriots. I was informed by Kelso, that wealthy merchants among the Dissenters were most lavish contributors to the funds of their sects, and to other benevolent objects. And that he had known instances in which men gave away annually twenty and thirty and even fifty per cent. of their income. Yet that is not by any means as assured as the incomes dependent on settlements. It will be my duty, if ever I am invested with the responsibility of these vast estates, to dispense their benefits over a wider area. One cannot help feeling pride at a position which enables a man to be so royal in the amount of his charities; but this is qualified by a sense of shame at a comparison of the sums thus given away by my father, with the magnificence of revenues outrivalling those of many a sovereign."

The value of these memoranda, which one may term Revelations of an Aristocrat, can hardly be overestimated. Indicating clearly *some*, shadowing forth *other* incidentia of our aristocratic institutions, and memorialised for us by one immediately concerned,— though at the time he was a hostile critic,—they raise some very grave and curious questions which the reader may resolve for himself.

※ ※
※

VII.—Land and Economy.

DRUMDRUM CASTLE might be denominated the feudal centre of the whole of Briggshire. It had been the effort of the Ffowlsmere ancestry, an effort in which the present Earl consistently followed them, to absorb into the vast estate from time to time the best of the holdings in the county; and so with patient watchfulness the Earl's steward purchased any property coming into the market: now one hundred acres, now ten, now three hundred. In this connection money was nothing to the Earl. He was able in the pursuit of a proud yet mean ambition to set economy political and private, at defiance, and much of this property had been purchased over the heads of energetic and improving farmers at prices that did not leave a profit of one per cent. to legitimate agriculture. The effect of these monopolizing tactics was to shut all the farmers in Briggshire within their own limits, denying them all hope of expansion. On the other hand, the Earl's objects were facilitated, since any extra energetic man desiring a larger field for his energies must needs sell out and seek it in another locality. One family had held its own against the Earl's predecessors with provoking obstinacy. Their estate was awkwardly interned in that of Drumdrum. They were poor, but they had Scotch Royal Blood in their veins (what Scotchman has not?) no matter how obtained. The estate, of nearly fifteen hundred acres, kept in a poor way the Laird and about fifty tenants of small holdings up and down the hills, on little spots carelessly tilled yet yielding to the simple people enough for their wants, and leaving them freedom to be happy. The Earl's agent, being a Scotchman, was the proper person to set to catch a Scotchman. He laid a trap for the Laird, who was known not to be flush of money. He won over the Laird's lawyer, to whom solemn injunctions had been given in all business transactions to avoid any contact with the Earl or his people. This man had been the constant medium of supplies to his impoverished client. He alone knew the ins and outs of his private affairs. The property was over-mortgaged, and the mortgages, one by one, had through his villanous agency come into the possession of the Earl's agent. When the time was ripe the mine exploded. The agent was able to write to Lord Ffowlsmere that now there was no hindrance to his seisin of Naboth's vineyard—though I need not say he did not write in those terms. The poor Laird went to Canada with his family. Notice to quit was served on all the tenants, numbering forty-five male or female householders, with one hundred and thirty-seven other adults and children. I would spare you the pain of reading a description of the anguish, the sorrow, the indignation, the despair kindled in one hundred and eighty-two human hearts by this economic proceeding. For the Earl afterwards wrote a pamphlet to prove that it was consistent with the soundest economy to sweep away these petty holdings and convert the whole estate into sheepwalks, a condition in which they were far more profitable, yielding more for less labour: or into deer forests which produced a larger rental, and venison for the London market! Unquestionably, if " economy "— that much wronged word—means the advantage of the rich, the Earl was right, and so long as he and his class can make laws, they will make them on that basis. But what of the greatest number? The hundred and eighty-two people who used to live contentedly, if wretchedly, on the soil; who might and ought to have been taught to improve their rude cultivation—to extend it around upon the rocky slopes—whose children at all events might have been educated to better things? Would to God the Earl were alive, and I could bring him face to face with the things that actually ensued upon his economic reforms—the fate of the living, the story of the dead! When they went away, to each of them was given, as a sop to public criticism and the Earl's conscience, a small sum sufficient to keep them for a few months, or convey them to Canada. The historian could run a bright flash through these pages, by narrating the luck of the men who chose this happy alternative. They found in

Canada a settlement of their own clan, in a rich country, with a glorious climate, and unlimited scope for the energies peculiar to their race. Now they or their children are wealthy. But of the rest? Government, in its wisdom, had provided neither information nor facilities to draw them to a colony. The greater number drifted to the large towns or fishing villages. In the towns they added to the crowds of searchers for employment, but the work they were accustomed to do was not always the work wanted in towns. The men were mostly driven to chance jobs, in which their great strength was useful; a few of the girls and boys obtained situations as servants: but the married women, the aged ones, the "uncanny" males and females—ah!—*they* gradually dwindled down to the point of starvation—and, curiously enough, at that point they died. The Earl has since then, from an opposite point, gone to meet them. It is possible he now wishes he had looked forward to that ugly contingency. The sheep and the deer meanwhile thrived vigorously on the spots that would have kept these people alive, while noble lords in company with gay young officers, vulgar parvenus and members of the Lower House, ranged and took their pleasure over the deserted heaths. I cannot trace out the long lines of sorrow that diverged from that single centre; the deaths, the diseases, the struggles, the poverty, the depreciation of bodies and souls—

> Ill fares the land, to hastening ills a prey,
> Where wealth accumulates and men decay.

May we not fitly stay a moment here and ask, *Is there a converse of this?* If such woe and need—such unsooth gain of wealth or pleasure to the rich at the expense of the poor,—at the expense of the truest, wisest, clearest *human* economy, ensue upon evictions from these little homesteads, what sorrow and wrong is there, what false economy, in permitting the operation of law and custom to shut out whole masses of the population from the hope of settling over the face of the land they live in. Will you, I pray, honestly suppress for a few minutes your rising prejudices, and forget your selfish interests, and ask yourself, whether it were not a wise and a just thing to aim at such legislation as should, without wrong to you or any other person, facilitate the establishment of cottier homes throughout this land, and the distribution of perishing people over our vast possessions beyond the seas? Is it not worth thinking and setting about for some time, even though the problem seem inscrutable and it may not be certain you will succeed? For what, think you, will kick the other scale?

VIII.—A Startling Lecture.

At Drumdrum Castle deer-stalking or grouse-shooting was the business of life. In the early morning a crowd of powerful and canny-looking keepers and beaters assembled—the keepers with their hounds in leash—and awaited the company that were to issue from the Castle gate, various in their mien and dress; some evidently no tyros at the sport; some as clearly inexperienced as they seemed by nature unfitted for a long stride over stony hills and heather braes, or for a clean shot with a steady hand when the time came. Yet it was a fine thing, as the signal bugle blew from the Castle wall, to see them bear away for a cool ten hours' toil, the weaker on sturdy little ponies, not a few in native or adopted Highland costume; it was a fine thing, I say, to see these men, from Cabinet Council and official desk, from Lombard Street, or even from the Bishops' Bench, start off in the bracing morn, expiring the unhealthy inhalations of metropolitan life and inspiring the glorious strengthfulness of a Scotch air. It was the best excuse to be afforded for a deer-forest that health to so many couched in its rough recesses. But I am bound to admit the excuse is a limited and lopsided one.

Such a party had one morning left the Castle, not the least of them the old Earl himself. Lord Bantam, never a keen sportsman, still loved to breathe the air and breast the hills, scenting the healthy ground-smell or the sweet heather. The factor, Macgruder, a celebrated deer-stalker, always managed the field, picking out the best stations for the crack shots, and with Caledonian shrewdness giving the bad ones nothing to do. Among these was the young lord, who found himself left like a sentinel behind a small cairn, with directions to keep his eye on the opposite hill, where an indistinct line in the heather denoted a track down which he was told he might hope to see a stag take its way. There he had stood for an hour half-dreaming, his gun loosely lying on his arm. Suddenly it was snatched from him, and he was confronted by a ragged, powerful old Highlander, with bonnet rakishly cocked; his long, strong, grizzly hair escaping beneath it; a face roughed and hewn by time, and care, and grief; and in its rugged cavities two fierce eyes fixed firmly on the startled young aristocrat.

"Who arr ye an whens arr ye that stan on Angus MacAngus's hairth-stane, my braw lad?" shouted the apparition in an unnatural voice, and with a strong Celtic accent, as he pointed to a moss-grown stone on which Lord Bantam was unconsciously standing: "Ye'll be the Airl's son, I'm thinking?"

"I am," said Bantam, his high breed recovering him in a moment, "and my party are not far off. What do you mean by taking my gun from me in that wild way? Give it me at once, or I'll call them on you."

"'T wad be yer dyin' call, my lad," replied the other coolly, giving his gun an uncomfortable twist in the direction of the young lord's red head; "Angus MacAngus is no' the man to be ta'en up for noethin."

"I tell you again, whoever you are, I am the Earl's son, and you had better not threaten or hurt me. I can bring twenty guns upon you in a minute."

Truth obliges me to say that Lord Bantam, though he uttered these bold words, did not look like a chieftain whose foot was on his native heath, and who felt confident as Roderick Dhu that his whistle would make the glen alive with followers.

HIGHLANDER. Haud still, till I hae a word or twa wi' ye, young mon; an' ye needna fear Angus Mac-Angus if ye'll only tak yer foot from Angus's hairth-stane, whare noo ye're standin'.

BANTAM. O, certainly, if it annoys you I will move; but why do you call this your hearth-stone? There never was a house here surely?

HIGHLANDER. Na hoose! na hoose! ye say? Ay, my lad, for mony a day whare noo ye see the nettle and the moss so thick amang the stones, was Angus Mac-Angus's home. A dour place it is noo, an' a douce place it was then. Mony a time I've sat an' look't into the bonny blaze on yon stane, wi' my auld Maggie knittin' at the ither side, an' Duncan, and Ewen, an' Tonald, an' my own little Maggie wi' hair as golden as the broom. O God, why did I live to see the like o' this!—cried he, throwing himself down on the deserted stone, and covering his face in his ragged plaid.

Lord Bantam's fear was gone, and curious sympathy took its place. He said kindly:

BANTAM. Come, my man, get up and tell me all about this. It is new to me. When did you live here?

HIGHLANDER. Even sinse you were born, young man,

this was a joyfu' home, wi' a good farm and dacent people about us yonder, and yonder, and yonder, where ye see the cairns. Anither laird we had then, a goot kind man he was too, God be wi' him wheriver he is; an' here ye see I had my wee croft, and there was Maggie's floure patch, an' the byre for the coo, an' here we lived from year's end to year's end, without sickness or sorrow, till that cursed old scourge, the Airl an' the Deil sent here, routed the poor laird from his heritage, an' then—an' then——

BANTAM. Turned you out!

HIGHLANDER. Ay! turned us out if ye will; pulled down our hooses, an' as ye see, put the hairths an' homes o' a hundred an' eighty souls under the feet o' the beasts and birds.

BANTAM. Is it possible? My father's steward? I never heard of this before. Why, it's clearly wrong. Where did you all go to?

HIGHLANDER. Go till? till the Deil most o' us, whare doubtless the factor and yer father and yersel will find us in goot time. Some went to Canada wi' the Laird, and some to Perth, an' some southwards.

BANTAM. Where did you go?

HIGHLANDER. I took my wife and bairns to Dondee, an' there I strove to keep them, but I wasna handy at toon work, and couldn't get a handfu'. My poor wee Maggie, she sickened first and pined away in thae crookt, crampt closes, an' my wife Maggie, she dwindled too——, an' they're all dead—they're all dead—an' may God call them to accoont that warked such awfu' grief—as na doobt He will.

The old man rubbed his brown hand across his eyes, and rising was about to hand the gun back to the young Lord, when his quick eye lighted on a fine buck, that had just topped the crest of the hill and was descending to the valley; in an instant the gun was at his shoulder, and at its report the animal leaped out from the hill and crashed down its side among the stones in the burn beneath. For a moment the excitement inspired the man; then he looked down with a dejected air upon the dead thing far beneath his feet.

"I could not help it," said he, "'twas a goot shot, an' Angus MacAngus has avenged on a poor beastie the wrong o' them that put it in his place; but I'm sorry it wasna Macgruder himsel'." Then giving Bantam the gun, and taking off his bonnet and standing before the heir, a weird yet majestic embodiment of wrong and sorrow, he said solemnly:

"I warn ye before God, that shall judge ye at the last, that should ye come to be Laird o' these braw lands, whare yer fellowmen an' their fathers, an' their fathers' fathers once freely enjoyed life and happiness, that ye remember *your* goot an' pleasure is no' all ye have to look till in what ye do. An unjust law may giv ye right to evic' an rob o' home and livin', poor, weak, innocent folk that can't resist ye: but there's a duty above right, an' a right above law, an' a God above a'—an' if ye wrong the poor an' escape yer punishment in this wurld, as ye are like to do, for it's a bad one, you must just make yer accoont to take it out elsewhares. *Woe, woe unto them that join hoose to hoose, that lay field to field, till there be no place; that they may be placed alone in the midst of the airth!*"

With that MacAngus plunged down a narrow bush-ridden cleft, familiar to him, and about which doubtless he led a wild life, leaving Lord Bantam to ponder on the singular lesson that had just been read to him, and to account to his friends for his magnificent shot.

PART V.

HOW HE BECAME A LEGISLATOR.

I.—A Vacancy.

IT had been agreed that our hero should take advantage of the first opening that offered in the serried ranks of the House of Commons. The theoretical ideal of a popular selection of the fittest man to represent an honest majority's views is rarely if ever attained in perhaps the only country in the world where a political Diogenes would think it worth while to look for it. In reality there is a practical juggle by which the converse has become the rule and the ideal an exception. It is, in nine cases out of ten, the member who chooses the constituency, not the constituency that selects the member. Externally of course the process seems perfect enough. There is a sudden spontaneous generation of enthusiasm in the minds of "leading men," which spreads its widening ripples over the surface of a constituency and ends in a demonstration to the world that the proper stone has found its bottom. But the antecedent action upon the leading men in which the motives originated are not exposed.

Indeed, so depraved has become our general political action, that though this is broadly suspected or perhaps recognised, popular feeling seems not to treat it with repulsion. How then are we to expect reform? This and all other approaches by means of legislation towards the higher electoral ideal can have no real effect unless the popular *morale* comes up to the level of it. Hence, in the present instance, a Peer, his son, and his excellent parliamentary agents Messrs. Shellers, consulted together with unaffected candour and the most naïve disregard of popular rights or perfect theories, how to impose Lord Bantam on the next constituency that happened to require a member. Lord Bantam agreed to hold himself ready to go anywhere: the solicitors held themselves prepared to do anything: and the Earl on his part held himself responsible, as a Cabinet minister, for giving the earliest notice of a prospective or actual vacancy. The constituencies were simply treated as squares in a chess-board—to be played upon. The coveted chance was afforded by the sudden demise of the honourable Member for Woodbury.

Woodbury, situated in the county of Gorseshire, was the centre of a busy district, agricultural and manufacturing. Many other towns had dropped down with their black canopies and eager hives of men upon the vales and hill-sides of the district, and this one was neither overweening in size nor conspicuous in importance. Yet with its Mayor and Council, its mace, its market-square, its town hall and assize courts, and its thirty policemen, it might justly claim to hold up its head among provincial towns. Of the 1,700 electors, 830 lived on property of a deceased millionnaire named Antrobus, whose trustees were a local banker and a noble member of the existing Government — the President of the Council. Mr. Antrobus died very wealthy—a friend of many a nobleman whom he had benefited at the rate of from twenty to fifty per cent. This town, containing an inadequate, ignorant and stupid number of British citizens, nevertheless in the usual English defiance of political equities, returned two members. When the first Reform Bill threw the nomination of those two persons out of the hands of the Antrobus interest, after two or three severe struggles between it and the radical division, a compact was tacitly made that each should return one of the members, and Woodbury may be said to have been then fairly represented. The Millionnaire interest had long been Fogy. The trustees were Prigs. The *cestui que trust* was a female and a minor. Popular opinion decidedly predominated in the borough if its action were unfettered; and the surviving member, a thorough Prig of the old stamp, had been returned avowedly as the nominee of the Millionnaire interest. Hence the two principal parties in the borough were the Millionnaire party and the people's party or "Independents." The Fogies were in a hopeless minority. When therefore the Independents lost their representative, they considered themselves entitled to nominate the candidate of the Popular party. I am compelled to add that the two sections lived with each other a Socrates and Xanthippe life, the reverse of happy for their political matrimony.

The two interests were managed in characteristically different ways. No sooner had the honourable member vacated the seat than the solicitor for the Millionnaire estate, who was in the confidence of the Treasury, and ot course had regular and rapid information, called into his office three or four Prigs " of the highest respectability," and announced that "the party in London" wished Lord Bantam, son and heir, etc., to stand, and that they could do nothing better than accept a candidate so distinguished. This solicitor's name was Pike, of Pike and Shrimp, and at that very interview he had in his pocket a cheque, enveloped in a letter from Messrs. Shellers retaining him as Lord Bantam's agent. This letter had reached him simultaneously with another from a distinguished authority by which he was informed of the vacancy. There could be no objection to so highly respectable a candidate on the part of such highly respectable constituents, the less when they were informed that the Millionnaire interest was to go in his favour. It was thereafter affirmed that Lord Bantam had been adopted as the Popular candidate by the local leaders of the party in Woodbury. The whole of this operation had been conducted on the strictest Prig principles.

Not many hours afterwards the walls were decorated

with a yellow placard, informing the electors that a Popular candidate of great eminence was coming and that his name would shortly be announced. Meanwhile an extravagant excitement in the best reception rooms of the Moon and Green Cheese, the great Millionnaire house, intimated to all Woodbury that *that* interest had settled on its man and was about to produce him forthwith.

II.—Diversities of Operations.

Mr. Blupell, Chemist, Congregationalist and Radical, had come out of his little back room to his shop, with his spectacles raised up upon his bald head, at the summons of another Radical of somewhat vagrant and electric political activity, who had rushed in to inform the leader of the Independent party that a vacancy had occurred. This was Nutt the baker. After him close came the little bow-legged Trades-unionist journeyman tailor, Tom Stretcher, with a head that seemed to be suffering from political hydrocephalus though indicating a careful abstention from the application of water to its exterior.

The three discussed the news.

"It's our turn to nominate," said Nutt. "You'd better get your coat on, Mr. Blupell, and let's go to Pike.

We ought to get the party together, and send a deputation to some one."

"I know who it must be," said Tom Stretcher, in a tone rather decided for a conference; "it will have to be a working man this time, Mr. Blupell. The Trades have resolved on that, I can assure you."

"What!" cried Nutt, "a working man? I think I see you getting a working man in with Mr. Pike's help! Why, he wouldn't look at a candidate without he had three or four thousand to spend on a contest."

"I know that, Mr. Nutt; but why need we go to Pike at all? It's our turn to nominate, ain't it?"

"Yes," said the experienced Blupell, "we may *nominate*, but the question is, whether they will accept our nominee. They are very strong now in the Council, and may take it into their heads, as this is a single vacancy, to try and pop a man in for the other seat—and there! as I'm a living man—what's that yellow placard Jack Traddles is pasting up yonder?"

In another minute Jack Traddles was in the shop, and a damp copy of the yellow placard was spread out upon the counter under the suggestive noses of the triumvirate.

"I half expected this," said Blupell, "when I heard your news. Pike passed me this morning without noticing me, though I'm sure he saw me. There's some mischief up, gentlemen. We must get to work at once. They have the start of us; though he can't get his man here before to-morrow night, I should think, if then. Let us put out a counter-notice at once, and hold a meeting at the Red Hoofs to-night."

In a short time a pink placard, from the establishment of the Radical printer, was being posted about Woodbury, calling upon the electors to "remember the compact, and to commit themselves to no candidate for the present."

War was declared.

Now the exact position of parties in the borough at this time was as follows. The Millionnaire party could count on 650 votes out of the 800 odd on the estate in any contest between Popular and Popular, the Fogy tenants always voting with the landholder, as under ordinary circumstances the only relic of party principle left for them to practise. They numbered about 140. The remainder of the Millionnaire tenants were not under discipline. There were 200 other Fogy voters in the town who could generally be relied on to vote one way, because they were kept well in hand by four or five principal employers of labour, specially by one Muggeridge, a brewer. About 370 voters were artisans and trades-unionists, all independent and Radical to the back-bone : 200 more respectable electors generally co-operated with the Independents. The balance consisted of moderate Liberals of little means, and some freemen ; and how they would all vote used to be a mystery until they had voted. To add to the complexity, the dissenting interest was very strong. Here were materials for some very pretty conjunctions.

Word was passed to all the leaders of the Independent party to be on the alert in the evening; and if in the early part of the day the Moon and Green Cheese had had its hysterics, in the evening the Red Hoofs had their turn of excitement. The long, low-ceiled room, with its old and rattling casements, its bulging walls, dismal paper and skirmishing long tables, was occupied by a lively committee.

During the afternoon, the barrister who happened to be nearest the scene of action, hearing of the opening, hurried to the spot and called on the leaders of the Independent section. Law, like nature, abhors a vacuum.

At the meeting, the Trades came out in unusual force. Tom Stretcher, who spoke with amazing nerve and pith, declared that to a man they had decided on putting up a candidate of their own class—a Mr. Ruggles of Ironchester. Several Populars—a manufacturer, two solicitors, a physician, and a retired captain, etc., all of whom professed extreme principles, protested however against this proposal. "Ruggles was a notorious agitator, and not a gentleman. What could he do in the House? How could he support himself? It would be ridiculous." Every word they uttered in this wise was driving in Ruggles's nails for him and securely fixing him in the affections of the artisans. The meeting broke into two divisions and adjourned till next evening, Mr. Blupell solemnly warning them that the breach would ruin their party; but then his only solution of the difficulty was that the rough majority should succumb to the genteel minority.

III.—Taking no Part in it.

THE election at Woodbury was not confined to Woodbury itself. A small share of its real importance concentrated there. The chief struggle was elsewhere. We now turn to this extra-mural portion of the conflict.

The death of Mr. Wilton, M.P., was announced in an evening journal and known at all the London Clubs within a few hours of the event. There were at the moment lounging about town nearly two hundred gentlemen of every rank, profession and state of wealth or impecuniosity, who were conscious of a heaven-ordained prescription that they should go into parliament. How many and various these beings that also stood and waited near the political sanctuary!—leeches longing to get a suck at the body politic—late members or ex-ministers eager to return to the political pastures out of which they had been driven—young gentlemen whose ambitious fathers desired to procure for them the opportunity of learning statemanship at the expense of the nation—barristers hungry for judgeships and willing to hold a perpetual brief for their party in the prospect of a handsome settlement for life—wealthy and vulgar tradesmen struggling for a social position—railway directors and stock-jobbing speculators plotting to make money out of the highest trusteeship of human experience—all with quick, keen noses scenting the carrion scent of the departed life, swooping down upon the place where the carcase had been, but certainly not worthy to be compared with eagles.

The same afternoon three peers with their sons, two railway directors, and half-a-dozen Queen's Counsel, who happened to be acquainted with Lord Haricot, the President of the Council and co-trustee of the Millionnaire estate, had called at Brook Street to solicit his influence. He was "out" to them all. To tell the truth he was closeted with Mr. Fugleman, the astute Whip of the Popular Party.

Mr. Fugleman was like all Whips. In describing one you describe another. To whatsoever side he belongs a Whip is a man who agrees to maintain no principles of his own—though he does not agree not to have them. He is at once the slave and the tyrant of party. To him looks the Prime Minister for information, organization, pressure, screw or cajolery: to him cringe the average members of his party for advice or assistance or interest. When his side is in power he is the dispenser of the smaller patronage; the middleman who goes between a minister desirous of purchasing a doubtful vote, and a member ready to sell his principles for place or position.

He is partially in the secrets of the Cabinet. It is his business to know the private aims of every man of his party. Representatives of doubtful constituencies look to him to procure appointments for unmanageable electors. To nine men out of ten on his side the house his word is law. When the ruck of members comes surging up to some critical division, from smoking-room, and library, and brandy and seltzer on the terrace he has been seen to stand and point with his finger to the sheep as they flocked towards him—and they have been seen to obey his signal. He pumps opinions whereby to guide the course of a time-serving government; he ascertains what policy is safest before any policy is announced; how far a ministry may go and no further.

Such an office is a study to a political critic. It seems so concrete and abject a recognition of the baseness of humanity. However, I never heard that any gentleman of stainless honour refused to accept so powerful a post. It is likely, under the *régime* of the Ballot, when members may require to be more careful of the opinion of their constituents, and constituencies may be less amenable to any influences other than those of principle and opinion, that this office may become an anomaly and cease to be possible.

Mr. Fugleman, the Prig Whip, was closeted with my Lord Haricot. I have said that the late millionnaire was a Fogy, and when he was alive his tenants, Prig, Fogy or Radical, had all voted consistently one way. He was a terribly tyrannical old disciplinarian, having risen from the lowest ranks. He would have turned in his grave had he known that his trustee was using the estate influence for the other party.

Said Lord Haricot:—

"I am willing and anxious to oblige Ffowlsmere. His family you know are connections of Lady Haricot. Besides, as the leader of the party in the Lords, he is entitled to anything I can do. I have heard the young fellow well spoken of for ability, though they say he is too 'earnest' a Radical. But all that will tone down. I would rather see a man before than behind his age, if he is not a fool."

"No doubt he'll tone down. Ffowlsmere makes a great point of getting him in. We sorely need some clever juniors just now."

"Well, you know I am only trustee of the property at Woodbury, and I have rarely interfered in the elections, never openly. The fact is, Pike, the agent, has had everything his own way; and you understand how to make him right," added the Lord President significantly. "Probably you have more acquaintance with the borough than I have. It's a nasty place to fight. There is a strong anti-Millionnaire party, and I think poor Wilton represented them. Won't they want to put up their man this time? There is a Doctor Dulcis, a Baptist, who has great influence,—the apostle of the sect in England I hear. Bantam must be sure to get him."

"O I know the details pretty well; we have ample information. I have always found the people troblesome, but Bantam's name and position will go down well with the Fogies, and if we get him out first we shall be able to put a screw on any other candidate, by charging him with dividing the party. In fact, I intend that Lord Bantam shall leave at once for the borough, and I only delayed until I had settled with you to put no other man in the field."

"I have no one to send. Look here—" and the Peer pointed to a row of cards on his table as a lacquey brought in another. "I have not seen one of 'em."

"One thing more. No doubt Ffowlsmere's agent will have made the estate agent all right; but to clinch the matter and give him ground with the people, I think it would be well for you to let him have a letter of introduction to Mr. Pike."

"Oh, you know I must not mix myself up with it at all. There'd be a deuce of a row; Cabinet Ministers interfering with the freedom of election, and that sort of thing."

"I think I can manage that for you," replied the wily Parliamentarian. "You could send a simple letter of introduction, saying, if you like, that you don't intervene at all. Pike will understand it perfectly, and it will have its effect."

The peer, an honest old fellow in his way, shrank even from this, but at length allowed himself to be persuaded by the Whip, who, to tell the truth, had his doubts about Woodbury. He wrote the following letter in autograph from a draft prepared by Mr. Fugleman.

Mr. Pike,—

Lord Bantam, son and heir of the Earl of Ffowlsmere, Secretary of State for Imperial Appendages, is, I am given to understand, likely to visit Woodbury on business connected with the election consequent on the death of your late lamented Member. He may need some advice from competent persons in the locality. I know no one better qualified to give him such advice than you, and I may say that any attentions you may pay him will be an obligation to myself.

With reference to the approaching election, I hope it will go off quietly. Of course I do not intend to take any part in it whatever.

Your faithful servant,
Haricot.

"It is very important not to lose this place in our present shaky condition," said Mr. Fugleman in taking leave of the peer. "But Ffowlsmere's desire to get in his son is very awkward for us. There's Ewing has been waiting for a seat these two years, and you know he fought West Cardshire twice. I promised him the next chance. Then there's Foley and Brampton and nearly a dozen others on the list, besides one of those d——d working men candidates, who are going to give us a lot of trouble I fear everywhere."

***

IV.—Fencing.

WHEN Mr. Fugleman reached his room at the Treasury, after his interview with Lord Haricot, his private secretary handed him the card of an Irish politician well known to be looking for a seat in the House, and informed him that two other gentlemen were waiting in the ante-room. One was Mr. Ewing, late M.P. for Biston, a man of business, specially valuable to the Ministry; for he never spoke, worked diligently on Committees, voted consistently with his party, and wielded a good deal of quiet influence. Mr. Fugleman was really vexed to be obliged in this instance to throw him.

"Well, Fugleman," said Ewing as he came in, "I think this chance will do. I've telegraphed to Pike, the Antrobus interest you know, and my agent has gone down. There can be no one in the way, this death is so unexpected."

"I'm sorry you have sent any one down, my dear fellow," replied his friend with some embarrassment.

"Why?" cried the other, somewhat dashed.

"Why, I've just heard, *privately*, you know, entirely a party secret, that young Bantam has been fixed upon by the Antrobus interest—old Haricot you know, trustee—relative of his mother's. I am not sure he has not gone down already. It would be awkward to interfere with such an arrangement."

"Young Bantam! Good Heavens, he's hardly of age—a red republican, and his father with a dozen boroughs in his hands. Why this is extortionate. I made certain of this chance. 'Pon my word, Fugleman, I don't think I shall stand it. Now I've begun I'll go on."

"I fear there is no chance," said the other. "You see my hands are tied. At all events, if you do go down to look at it, promise me you won't divide the party."

"Not to let in a Fogy. Good-bye for the present."

"Good-bye," said Fugleman, "I will see what can be done for you."

He would have more accurately expressed it had he said that he would see his friend done for.

The other gentleman was shown in: Mr. Tilson—contested Shoeborough, Titmouse, Rustiton—all unsuccessfully—therefore supposed to have immense claims on the party.

"Ah, Tilson! Anything up! What's the news from Shoeborough? I hope you are nursing it carefully?"

"Oh yes, my subscriptions are all paid regularly, but I have come to you about Woodbury. I ought to have a chance there. My cousin Richey the agricultural machine maker has a great deal of influence, and as a dissenter I should do well in the borough. My agent went down by the last train. Is any one else in the field?"

"Why, yes. Ewing is talking of going down, and he's a very strong man anywhere, and we very much want him in the House."

"Any one else?"

"Two or three are spoken of, but I shall know more to-morrow. Will you come in in the afternoon?"

The Whip was perplexed, and needed time for reflection. This man with a cousin a local manufacturer was not a comfortable interpellant and too important to be flouted.

"I'm afraid that will leave it very late," said Mr. Tilson, "but I depend on you to do your best for me."

This utterly gratuitous expression of confidence made the Whip wince, and rather annoyed him.

V.—Party Tactics.

FIVE minutes later a Treasury messenger in a hansom was conveying to our hero the Lord President's letter with a message to be off by the next train as there was likely to be opposition; and he was warned to avoid travelling with Mr. Ewing should he be going by the same train.

Mr. Fugleman then put on his hat and went to the office of the Prig attorneys, Messrs. Pivots, in many respects the head-quarters of the party organization throughout the kingdom. The elder Mr. Pivot was virtually the Whip's factotum. He was in all the electoral and not a few of the political secrets of the party—a man whose face was a mask, whose head was a geometric maze whereof he only held the skein; a man of the world, polished and brilliant: of vast experience, able, astute, inscrutable. There were self-restraint and hidden tact in the very cut of his coat. What tales could he have told of human ambitions and failures, of human follies and foibles! He sat in a room from which by merely ringing a bell he could communicate almost directly with any part of the kingdom. In an adjacent chamber half a dozen busy and silent clerks wrote and filed correspondence, conned reports, abstracted or minuted information contained in letters and newspapers. It was a wonder that an organization so elaborate and so perfect did not preserve more harmony than was at that time commonly apparent in the ranks of the party. It is just possible that it may have been too mechanical in its movements and not sufficiently adaptive or tactical —but such a criticism may be deemed impertinent and I withdraw it. How perfect the clerical work was, appeared when the Whip entered and taking a chair evidently retained for him said:

"Pivot, what do we know about Woodbury?"

PARTY TACTICS.

Mr. Pivot rang a bell. A clerk entered.

"Bring in the electoral note-book for Gorseshire."

A large volume was brought in, and opened at a page headed Woodbury, opposite which was a map of the borough, with certain portions indicating the various "interests" coloured. Mr. Fugleman sat perusing a carefully compiled account of the voters, properties and influences of that constituency.

"I see the Wesleyans are strong down there. Lord Bantam is rather a free-thinker from what I hear. He must be cautioned to keep his opinions to himself."

"I don't think he'll have any difficulty with them," said Mr. Pivot; "but I have just received a telegram from Pike. A barrister with some local influence named Heneage is already canvassing the borough, and the Trades are talking of a candidate of their own, Ruggles of Ironchester. If either of them stands, the party will be split, and a Fogy may have a chance."

"Hum! You had better send word to Sheller at once. He's a shrewd fellow, and may be able to stave off the workman. But here's Ewing gone down already, and Tilson talking of going. I see by this memorandum, Richey, his cousin, 'controls some fifty to eighty votes, principally among small householders.' I put Tilson off till to-morrow; but really I'm puzzled to know how to deal with him, for we must have Richey's support at any cost."

"A nice mess they'll make of it," said Pivot. "We must stop this at once or the borough is lost."

"Well what are we to do?"

"You can manage Tilson if he is determined, and win his cousin's interest at the same time. He only wants a seat to make good his claim to an appointment. That Stickleback Bank business affected him very considerably and he has claims on the party. You might offer him the governorship of Mungopore."

"That I know Lord Ffowlesmere has already promised to Norton. But he can give him the next vacancy. There's British Liana where the governors don't stay very long. You must see him to-night, and arrange it. We cannot afford to let him go down."

"I don't think there's much fear of Ewing," said the sagacious Pivot. "He's too good a man to fight a useless contest. It is these pestilent barristers and pauper politicians and ambitious working men that give us so much trouble. Heneage is the most dangerous feature against the young lord. True he is a Popular, but he's nobody. Then these barristers never like to take their teeth out when they have once laid hold, unless they are offered a bite at better meat; and he is altogether too young for an appointment. If it came to a duel between Bantam and Ruggles, there would be little doubt of the result with the Fogy vote for us; but that fellow Heneage will certainly weaken our party. His family stands well in the whole county."

That evening Mr. Pivot saw Mr. Tilson at his own house. When he came away Mr. Pivot understood that

Mr. Tilson did not intend to stand for Woodbury, and Mr. Tilson understood that it had for some time been the intention of the Government, in consideration of his past services, to confer on him a Colonial governorship, a desire to be put into execution on the occurrence of the next vacancy; the two understandings being also understood to be perfectly independent of each other. Mr. Tilson withdrew his agent from the borough because Mr. Pivot had conclusively proved to him that the field was already occupied by Lord Bantam; and Mr. Pivot incidentally disclosed to Mr. Tilson the aforesaid good intentions of the Ministry, which made it hardly worth while for Mr. Tilson to go into the House.

I should like to know what the Colony, to whose lot happened to fall this broken politician, would have thought of the method in which the cards of its government were shuffled; or whether any empire under heaven could long maintain its position, if so grave a business as the selection of rulers for its matchless provinces were conducted in so scurvy a manner?

* *
*

VI.—Marching Orders.

MR. SHELLER was certainly a shrewd man at an election. For thirty years he had been managing electoral contests, county and borough, open and close, pure and the reverse. He knew the history of every English constituency, the means and influences required in each. We have already seen that his provisional retainer on Lord Bantam's behalf was in Mr. Pike's pocket almost whilst the deceased member was yet warm. Now it was a cardinal rule of Mr. Sheller's business that he never attended to any of it himself. He did everything by proxy, and proxy always had the responsibility. In the present case, for so great a client, unlimited means, &c., &c., Mr. Sheller would if necessary have gone a long way, but he acted with his usual caution. He sent for the cleverest man on his staff; named, by a strange perversion, Simpleton.

"Simpleton," said Mr. Sheller, looking straight into the shrewd face of the agent, with its puckered mouth, resolute nose and chin, crow-footed temples, all transfigured by a bland smile, "you are to leave town by five-forty train for Woodbury. Vacancy caused by death of Charles Peter Wilton, Esquire. Our candidate is Lord Bantam, only son of the Right Honourable the Earl of Ffowlsmere. Pure Prig interest. You know the borough. You worked it in the religious interest for the late Mr. Jeremiah Nye, Baptist and shipowner. They say there is to be a Trades' Candidate. If so all your tact will be required. I need not tell you, Mr. Simpleton, that no effort must be spared—*no effort*, you understand, Mr. Simpleton—to return our client. I have complete confidence in you. I therefore place the whole matter in your hands. I need not remark that money is of no consequence to our client—that is, for any legitimate expense—any legitimate expense," said Mr. Sheller, tapping his snuff-box on the table, with stern emphasis, and steadily gazing into Mr. Simpleton's eyes, which bore the examination with equal steadiness. "Three thousand pounds will be placed to your credit at Messrs. Bentley and Thurston's bank, and I shall expect a careful and exact account of every penny, Mr. Simpleton. The greatest caution must be observed, for I need not tell you this is a very important client, Mr. Simpleton—a most important client, Mr. Simpleton— *a client that ought never to fail, Mr. Simpleton!* You will no doubt be too occupied to communicate with me, Mr. Simpleton; and should any further funds be required, you will telegraph direct to Earl Ffowlsmere's solicitors, Messrs. Hawke, **Hawke** and Peckham, if you please. There is £100 in five pound notes, Mr. Simpleton. Be good enough to count it and give me a receipt. Thank you. Good day and good luck to you, Mr. Simpleton."

As Mr. Simpleton and his small brown portmanteau drove to the station where he was to meet Lord Bantam, he winked at the cabman's back and smiled to himself.

"A—cautious bird, old Sheller—a—*very*—cautious bird. He means Lord Bantam to be returned *at—all— events*, and he doesn't want to know anything about it. Very well, Mr. Sheller. If possible, Lord Bantam shall be returned at all events, and you shall not know anything about it. You shall have a careful account of every penny,—of course you shall, Mr. Sheller. Cautious bird—a—very—cautious bird. Ha! Ha!"

The cabman pulled up. "I beg your pardon, sir. What did you say?"

"Nothing. Oh! nothing—," responded he, smiling. "I was blowing my nose.—A *very* cautious bird."

* * *

VII.—Too much of a Good Thing.

WE will return in the train with Lord Bantam and Mr. Simpleton to the borough of Woodbury. While they, received by Mr. Pike and partner, two local magnates and a respectable company of the Millionnaire tenants, entered a carriage and drove in state to the Moon and Green Cheese, let us ascertain what has been doing in the interval of our absence. Mr. Heneage, the barrister, was well known to the Woodburyites as one of the leading juniors on the Circuit. His wife was the daughter of a Squire who lived on a handsome estate some five miles out of the place. With a barrister's alacrity, he set to work and earwigged several important members of the Independent party. Availing himself with some skill, of the point that it was their turn to nominate a candidate; while he set them strongly against Pike for attempting to usurp the place of party dictator, he had succeeded in gaining considerable support. On the other hand, an afternoon parliamentary train had brought in from Ironchester the notorious Ruggles, and to meet and escort him to his humble lodging, the Trades of Woodbury had turned out in a body, losing half a day. A City of London warehouseman of the Baptist persuasion and enormous wealth had also come down, and was endeavouring to form among his co-religionists the basis for a further raid among the secularists. There was no lack of candidates.

Blupell was exercised beyond endurance. He asked what wickedness the town had committed to be so deluged with talents. When Heneage came, then Ruggles came, then Tomkins came; his patience gave way, and he retired to bitter reflections in his back-room. In the evening the various head-quarters were in full blast. Lord Bantam was introduced to about a hundred of his supporters at his inn. The Independents had their meeting—a very stormy one, the effect of which, instead of promoting harmony, was to increase the discord. Most of the respectables declared for Mr. Heneage; the Baptists said they should hold off at present in favour of Mr. Tomkins, and the Trades swore that Ruggles or a Fogy should have their votes; upbraiding the others for their want of liberality in not yielding to the majority and adopting a working-man.

Next morning at eight o'clock Lord Bantam's address

was upon all the walls. At nine o'clock the bill-sticker of the Trades pasted Mr. Ruggles's address over the placards of the noble lord. At ten o'clock an address was issued by Mr. Heneage, "emboldened by the almost unanimous wish of the electors," and relying on his "long and intimate connections with the borough." At eleven o'clock a placard announced a meeting in the evening to hear an address from Mr. Tomkins. The electors were bewildered. The Freemen alone retained their composure. They lounged leisurely in the market-place, with hope beaming softly in their faces as they contemplated the coming struggle.

In his address, the young lord, spite of the remonstrances of Mr. Simpleton, introduced a distinct appeal to the democracy. He declared "his sympathies to be with those who felt that the time was rapidly approaching for the removal of many of the restrictions on land, on labour and on the conscience; and that it was not unlikely that organic changes in the Constitution would be necessary preludes to those great reforms."

Mr. Simpleton and Mr. Pike calculated that under ordinary circumstances this sentence ought to lose him a hundred votes; but they comforted themselves that there was a compensating balance in his illustrious wealth and station. Some of the Trades even spoke of him approvingly.

Mr. Ewing did not appear. His agent met him at the station, and deterred him from alighting or exposing himself. He entered the train with him, having taken tickets to the next town. He was too shrewd to let his client's name slip into the newspapers connected with a hopeless candidature.

VIII.—An Election Manœuvre.

THE experienced Mr. Pike, the experienced Mr. Shrimp, and the experienced Mr. Simpleton, held a consultation. They had their man in the field, but forty-eight hours had completely changed its aspect. The unexpected attitude of the Trades and the appearance of Mr. Heneage, were both vexatious incidents. Mr. Pike knew perfectly well, he had found it out by experience in the municipal elections, that the Trades' influence determinately put forth was over many of the Millionnaire tenants stronger than his own, and that a cool half hundred of his voters and others whom he had hoped to influence for Lord Bantam would, whatever the consequences, assuredly go for Ruggles. Again, a number of the most respectable Millionnaire supporters would be led by local sympathy to adopt Heneage—thus, as he expressed it, "cutting off the young lord's tail at both ends;" and now, Mr. Simpleton having reviewed the field, pronounced it a certainty that a Fogy would be started if they did not clear away one or other of the rivals in twenty-four hours. After an animated consultation, they resolved to adopt a bold and original course suggested by Simpleton. A huge blue placard, without printer's name, shortly afterwards illuminated the walls and shop windows of the town. It was in these words:—

> FOGY ELECTORS!
> RESERVE YOUR PROMISES. AN EMINENT
> FOGY CANDIDATE
> IS COMING!

About an hour after its appearance Mr. Pike procured a copy and went over to Blupell the apothecary. That person received him with reserve.

PIKE. Look here, Mr. Blupell (unfolding the placard).

BLUPELL. Ah!—well, I suppose now you'll see your way to withdraw your man.

PIKE. Don't be in such a hurry, my dear fellow. I of course, like yourself and the whole Popular party, will do anything rather than let in a Fogy. I came to consult with you about the action we should take. We ought to agree upon a candidate without further delay.

BLUPELL. If you really have come to consult with me about it, Mr. Pike, I have but one course to recommend, the only honest and straightforward one, and that perhaps won't suit you; *withdraw your man.* I must say it is rather cool of you, after breaking a well-understood compact by bringing in a man without notice to any of us, to come and say we ought to agree. You never took the proper way to make us agree, which was to call a meeting of the party.

PIKE. Oh! I see you are clearly labouring under a misunderstanding. Lord Bantam is here to appeal to all classes. I can answer for it he is willing to submit his candidature to the whole party.

BLUPELL. Why did you not do this at first? We have no personal objection to him; indeed, I rather like him. He is more independent than his supporters; but we do object to your dictating to the borough and bringing a man down without consulting with the rest of us.

PIKE. Well, I may have made a mistake, but I am anxious to rectify it. We must do so at once. I have reason to believe that a Fogy, very highly connected, will be brought forward, and unless we all pull together we shall lose the seat.

BLUPELL. And serve you right if we do, Mr. Pike. I am not going to help you out of the scrape. I have promised Mr. Heneage my support this morning—there!

PIKE. Very well, Mr. Blupell. I shall never forget this.

BLUPELL. You do me an honour.

Pike's face was a study as he turned out of the chemist's shop. Blupell's decision was a blow in itself, and was besides an indication of more serious defection.

He crossed the High Street, and went down it to the tailor's shop, where Mr. Thomas Stretcher, presiding over eight brother-snips, constituted with them one man, according to the proverb. Mr. Pike had hitherto ignored Mr. Stretcher very much in all his political action. It was rather a humiliation to be obliged to go to him, but a retainer is very exacting. On asking for the Unionist he was referred to a back yard, thence up a rickety staircase, thence along an intoxicated passage, and finally he went unexpectedly down a step through a door and into a circle of cross-legged trades-unionists busily plying their needles.

"Oh! ah! Mr. Stretcher," said Pike; "could I speak to you a moment?"

"Yes," said Stretcher, quietly passing his goose down the selvage of a waistcoat he was making; "you can speak to me, Mr. Pike, I s'pose. It's a free country."

"Ha! ha! yes. Very good; but I want to say a few wards to you in private."

"No need to talk in private, Mr. Pike. I guess your business well enough, and we're all friends here. If you've got anything to say, say it out like a man. I've no time to spare gossiping in whispers with you or any one else in hours."

Even Mr. Pike's experience was unequal to talking privately to a man in the hearing of eight persons. However, he made the best of it.

"Well," said he, "I agree with you; the more who hear me, the better. We all have one aim. Have you seen this?" he contined, seating himself in a confidential way on the doorstep, and opening up the placard. The men looked up and read in silence, then went on with their work. "This shows what will happen, if our party is not united."

"*Our* party, Mr. Pike?" said Tom Stretcher; "what is *our* party? You represent the land and money interest; we, the claims of labour. You have your young lord, with his spurious liberalism, very like your own, with a good deal of soft sawder for us poor working men when we can be useful to you, but precious little to say or do when the time comes to help us. You represent the landlord screw; we are the true freemen. No; we have ceased to lean on that reed: our hands have been pierced often enough already. There's an instance of it in your hole-and-corner way of bringing this young lord down into the borough. You have gone and brought him here without asking any questions of us, and we have nothing to do with him, and don't mean to."

THE $\frac{8}{9}$ths. Hear, hear!

STRETCHER *(continuing).* We've had enough dictation from the Millionnaire side — a great deal too much. But the day of power for the people is coming, and all these tyrannical interests will have to succumb to the rising sovereign. It is time we should have representation of our own class in a Parliament composed of landowners, capitalists and blood-sucking professionals; and we mean to strike out a line for ourselves. The Trades are going for a man of their own—Mr. Ruggles, and depend upon it we shall return him or a Fogy.

PIKE. That is exactly what I wanted to know and to speak about. I recognise the working-men's claims to the full; so does my client. I only ask that we should take means to ascertain our relative strength, and when that is discovered, let us unite the whole party on one candidate. If Mr. Ruggles is decided upon, why you can rely on the whole of us to assist you.

STRETCHER. No we can't. It's no use sitting there and telling lies, Mr. Pike. We know as well as you do that you and all like you would rather vote for a Fogy than a working man, and we can see that if you want us to go into negotiations for a settlement it is with the intention on your part of settling it one way. We understand you. You have had your fee and you must earn it. We are looking for a representative; you are working for a client.

Mr. Pike's face was a browner study than before. It was useless for him to vent his rage upon nine Unionists in a small back room eighty feet from the front door; so he withdrew, and had the mortification to hear a hearty outburst of laughter as he went down the long passage.

The placard trick had turned out a failure.

In the evening Mr. Tomkins held what was termed an enthusiastic meeting, and no doubt to a superficial observer would have appeared so; but three-fourths of the crowd was composed of Fogies or trades-unionists or freemen, anxious to draw another champion into the *mêlée*.

※ ※
※

IX.—A Fogy Candidate.

WHILE the Populars were thus crystallising into organisms, representing the healthy variety of their opinions or their personal and local piques, a few shrewd Obstructives in the borough opened communication with headquarters. They had come to the conclusion that if any two of the existing candidates went to the poll, there was a fair chance for a Fogy; and if all three persisted in their candidature the Obstructive success was certain. Their tactics were in extreme contrast with those of their opponents. A committee of a dozen met privately at the house of Mr. Muggeridge the brewer. The rest of the party contentedly awaited their decision and not a word of their counsels escaped to the other side. They themselves knew every move of the Populars almost as soon as it was made. In applying to the party leaders in London to procure them a candidate, they warned them that their policy was not to produce him till a late hour. Mr. Pike heard of the meetings, and felt sure there was danger in the air, but he could discover nothing. Simpleton wrote to Mr. Fugleman, urging him to take means to draw off Heneage. Lord Bantam and Heneage canvassed vigorously, and Ruggles addressed the electors every evening.

Mr. Pivot's ingenuity exhausted itself in trying to find a solution of this electoral knot. Heneage was offered a

Recordership. His vanity, however, accepted this as a proof how dangerous he was, and he refused it. The writ was issued; but Pike being the town-clerk, and the mayor an Antrobus man, it was clear the election would be delayed till the latest moment. No sooner was the writ proclaimed, than the Fogy mine was sprung. The walls of Woodbury effloresced in blue placards, informing the Obstructive electors that a candidate was coming. He duly arrived by the afternoon train. Mr. Muggeridge, with his friends and a large body of freemen, who now saw their brightest hopes about to be realised, received him with enthusiasm at the railway station. He was a young honourable—a captain in the army, cousin to a peer whose splendid domain was the resort of the townsfolk. No sooner had he reached the borough than significant circumstances were noted by experienced observers on the Popular side. His address was issued—with a compliment to the trades-unionists—referring to his high lineage, and the proximity of one of the estates of his brother, and to his service in Her Majesty's livery (not using that word). It declared him to be a moderate Fogy, "desirous of advancing, at a pace consistent with safety, without hazarding the Crown, the Church, or the Constitution, the highest interests of the working man."

He pronounced against the ballot, but was in favour of giving to the artisan his legitimate rights.

On these grounds he requested to be returned, and began an energetic canvass of the borough.

Another significant circumstance was the unwonted facility of credit for draught ale offered by the publicans, and the vast number of drunken persons who paraded the streets, uttering warm exclamations of adherence to Captain Cavendishe "ash she besht man."

More significant still was the coolness exhibited by numbers of persons—previously favourable to one or other of the Popular candidates—whose eyes had been opened to their errors by the appearance of the young Captain.

Mr. Pivot himself arrived in Woodbury by the train succeeding that which had conveyed the Honourable Captain Cavendishe. He had letters of introduction from the Whip to various tried friends. One from Tilson to his manufacturer cousin; and others from a certain peer of the realm to the agent of a certain estate and to Mr. Richey.

***

X.—Electoral Skirmishing.

MR. PIVOT had seen Lord Bantam and his agents, and had taken the bearings of the position. To his experienced eye it looked very *blue* in more senses than one. Tilson's cousin had been visited by the young lord, but was hanging fire. Mr. Simpleton had come to the conclusion that he meant to support Mr. Heneage, who was known to be plying him with personal and family influences. Mr. Richey belonged to the Independent party in the borough, and felt himself much aggrieved at the assumption of Mr. Pike in introducing, without consulting that party, a candidate who was clearly a Ministerial "bantling"—this was Mr. Richey's mild play on the young lord's name. Had the compliment of consulting Mr. Richey been paid to him before Lord Bantam's arrival, there can be no doubt he would have esteemed him the most eligible candidate in the world; so seriously is our judgment affected by the method of presenting things.

When Mr. Pivot called upon Mr. Richey he was politely but drily received.

"I have had a very long and pressing letter," said the engineer frankly, "from Tilson, and am glad to hear he has been so well provided for. I have had to help him a little lately. I wish I could in return aid his views and yours, consistently with my conscience; but of course you would not wish my judgment to be warped by any generosity of the Government to a relative of mine."

"Oh! certainly not," responded Mr. Pivot. "These matters should always be kept entirely distinct."

"Yes," repeated the other, "these matters should always be kept entirely distinct. And I propose to keep them distinct. Tilson has done the Government good service in the past, and it is for that no doubt they have given him his reward. I may as well say at once, I this morning came to the determination to support my friend Mr. Heneage."

Mr. Pivot expressed his regret, affirmed the hopelessness of the barrister's chance, explained the position of the party, the importance of returning Lord Bantam, who was a most brilliant and promising young man——

"Rather extreme, eh?" hinted Mr. Richey.

——Extreme in theory, but practically under his father's able influence and the necessities of his fortune, of a safe conservative spirit. It had been quite taken for granted that Mr. Richey would as usual support the Government and use his immense influence in helping to heal the divisions in the party. Already was it becoming too late to do it since the Fogy was in the field. He urged Mr. Richey to reconsider his determination. Lord Bantam was the Government candidate, and he might reckon that he had the support of Lord Haricot, who had given him a letter to Mr. Pike, the Antrobus agent.

Mr. Richey was intractable. He declined to change his mind. Then Pivot produced Mr. Tilson's introduction, containing an urgent appeal to his relative, and a letter from Lord Haricot, as an old friend and one who in his trust capacity had had considerable dealings with Mr. Richey's firm, asking him to support "the party candidate" and the son of a most intimate friend. Mr. Richey's father and father's father had been manufacturers in Woodbury, and Mr. Richey was a proud-nosed man. His nostrils dilated when he read this letter. Bowing stiffly to Mr. Pivot he told him he could not see his way to support Lord Bantam. Mr. Pivot took his leave.

He was more fortunate in his next venture. Mr. Tomkins was still in the way; and Mr. Tomkins's vanity was not hard to touch.

By an adroit use of combined promise and flattery, the Treasury agent succeeded in imbuing Tomkins with the notion that he was the most dangerous rival in the field and that his retirement would turn the election. This to Tomkins was next best thing to getting in himself, and in the proud consciousness of his importance, he at once offered his best support and his influence among the Dissenters to the Ministerial candidate. He was introduced to Lord Bantam; whereupon his services were put in requisition to bring the young lord into communication with the noted Baptist preacher, Dr. Dulcis.

XI.—Canvassing Extraordinary.

DR. DULCIS was one of the most remarkable of living Dissenters. A profound theologian, a singularly ripe and elegant scholar, a powerful rhetorician, eloquent, refined, a man of science, he had shed the rays of his genius far beyond the atmosphere of his rather narrow denomination. Few men of letters or of science were unacquainted with the brilliant and industrious minister, and he won their affection, along with their regard, by the strangely magnetic attraction of his manner. Circumscribed as hasty opinion would have deemed his Calvinistic creed, he displayed towards all men the broadest kindliness, while he boldly indicated by word and life where his own sheet-anchor was fixed. His facile pen played with an almost bewitching skilfulness, procuring for him a reputation high among the literary men of his day. It was no wonder that a man of such qualities should be a man of influence, and he was looked upon by the agents, in their business-like-estimate, as one of their best "cards."

Accordingly, under Mr. Tomkins's "ægis," as he called it, Lord Bantam and Mr. Simpleton waited upon the minister. He was a man of some means—of which his dwelling, an old-fashioned town residence, with a good walled garden in the rear—gave evidence.

As they entered the house they heard the tones of an organ. The maid opened a door into the room from which the sounds proceeded. Several voices were singing a quaint tune; and Lord Bantam, staying the servant's announcement, signed to his companions to pause and listen. The scene before them at the end of the large room was engaging. A fair-faced girl, with a crown of golden hair, sat at the organ, to which a tall, thin, but not ungraceful man—evidently Dr. Dulcis—was energetically supplying breath while he used up his own. Round them were grouped three or four children, ranging in age from four to thirteen, and all were singing clearly and heartily to a Scotch melody the words—

> How great's the goodness Thou for them
>   That fear Thee keep'st in store;
> And wrought'st for them that trust in Thee,
>   The sons of men before!
>
> In secret of Thy presence Thou
>   Shalt hide them from man's pride;
> From strife of tongues Thou closely shalt,
>   As in a tent, them hide.
>
> All praise and thanks be to the Lord;
>   For He hath magnified
> His wondrous love to me within
>   A city fortified.
>
> For from thine eyes cut off I am,
>   I in my haste had said,
> My voice yet heard'st Thou, when to Thee
>   With cries——

At this point a velvet-coated little cherub, rolling his eyes round the room, happened to fix them on the strangers at the door, whereupon dropping the line, he shouted, "Papa, look!"

Dr. Dulcis turned from his labours and came forward. His face was flushed with exertion, but, endued as he was with all the self-possession of a gentleman, he exceedingly impressed the young lord by the dignity of his manner.

"You find me at a favourite amusement, my lord,"

said he, as if unconscious of the kindly irony which his term for the occupation of singing such uncouth verses suggested to the minds of his hearers; "we are all fond of singing, and specially fond of some of those old Scotch versions which preserve so much of the ruggedness and simplicity of the original. These verses afforded consolation to very different men. Luther, a man of action, used to dwell with pleasure on that nineteenth verse; and the next was a favourite one of Melancthon, whose gentle mind was peculiarly sensitive to the 'strife of tongues.'"

It is needless to say that this opening rather placed the agent outside the conversation, but the young lord took it up very cordially. *Apropos* of the Psalms, he forthwith plunged into a discussion on the Hebraism of Milton, and was astonished by the acute and brilliant comments made by his interlocutor. The agent was peculiarly vexed; he deemed this a sheer waste of time; he was a man of the world in a sense, but his wisdom stopped at a low level. He did not know, what Lord Bantam's higher instincts told him, that with the man before him he was doing more good by this conversation than by several hours of political babble. At length the doctor himself came to the point.

"I am very glad to see you, my lord," said he, "for your movements have not been without interest to me. Your boldness in casting off the restraints of class-interest, in your circumstances and at so early an age, has, if you pardon the liberty I take in expressing it, won my preliminary regard."

"I am for right and justice," said the noble proletarian; "a right and justice based, I believe, on the original principles of a great Teacher, whom you honour as a divine prophet, and I as a human philosopher of singular insight and power. In the early simplicity of His disciples, before casuistic and transcendental refinement had been introduced by speculative theorists like Paul, the tendency of the followers of Christ was to that perfect Commune which the purest and most advanced philosophy of this day regards as the highest ideal of human social organization."

The agent was stupefied. Dr. Dulcis seemed to overlook the combination of ungracious inferences involved in the young man's speech—the result of that intellectual arrogance which is the most common and intolerable of our University affectations. He said, quietly,

"We could hardly discuss at this time all the points raised by your lordship. I of course regard them in a different light and with another judgment. What I am happy to see is that you express broad and liberal opinions—such as in my belief must always when sincerely held and freely expressed tend to bring truth out of darkness and fix it in human conduct. Politically I am inclined to agree with you that there is much to be learned in modern economic polity, from the simple social principles of Christ; but I am afraid it is dangerous to say so. Men are unhappily not prepared for the millennium."

"But," intruded the business-like Mr. Simpleton, "do you think, Dr. Dulcis, you can give his lordship your support at this election?"

"I think I can," said the doctor; "and if you should be returned, as I hope you may be, perhaps we shall have frequent opportunities of comparing notes on many important subjects."

The young lord with difficulty drew himself away from the charming Dissenter to the harassing and degrading business of canvassing. There is probably no occupation, short of a crime, more demoralising—and none certainly so disheartening, as the door to door mendicancy of a candidate for the honour of representing a borough in the Parliament of these kingdoms.

XII.—Inconvenient Results of Popular Reform.

MR. PIVOT's next move was towards the democracy. He was in Woodbury, not to secure the return of a Popular but to obtain a seat for a Government nominee. To checkmate the dangerous barrister, it was essential that the Trades-unionist should first be dismissed the field. So Mr. Pivot called upon Ruggles. They had met before. Ruggles was an agitator, and had taken part in many contests on behalf of democratic candidates, whose gratitude vanished with their success. His rude and straightforward abilities were special antipathies of the Treasury agent.

"Ha! Mr. Pivot," said the Unionist, "are you down here? There's sure to be some mischief up. You are not come to help me I know."

"I am down here," said the other blandly, "to help the party. With this excess of Popular candidates the party will go to the wall. Is there no way of negotiating a compromise? Take me into your confidence."

"If I took you in there," said Ruffles, "you would soon take me in another way I'm thinking. However, I'll be frank with you. There *is* one negotiation that will answer."

"What's that?" asked the other.

"Withdraw the other candidates——"

"Oh! I have no influence over them whatever."

"Yes you have, Mr. Pivot, pardon *me*. The Treasury has ways of getting rid of candidates when they want to get in a gentleman. Let them show their sincerity towards us by helping me to the seat now there is a good chance of returning me."

"Impossible," said Pivot. "Lord Bantam has the Antrobus influence and you cannot expect him to withdraw, nor can you offer him any inducements to do so. As for Mr. Heneage, I understand he is unmanageable."

"Of course. He is a barrister looking for place," said Ruggles bitterly.

"Well, now, Ruggles," said Pivot, "you and I have worked together, and understand each other——"

"Do we?" interjected the shoemaker in an undertone.

"And really, my dear fellow, such a town as this is not the place for you. You are a reasonable man, and have sense enough to see that this is an aristocratic and middle-class borough, and such people need educating up to the point of adopting a working-man candidate. I admit the stupidity of their prejudice, but as a practical man I entreat you to consider how hopeless it is to overcome it. If you will show me any borough in which there is a sufficient number of working men to give you a chance, honour bright, I promise you the support of the Treasury, and the money shall be found."

"Stay a minute," said the unruly Ruggles; "you propose to return me somewhere by *working men*. I am fighting for a wider principle than the mere return of a working man by working men. We are insisting that there ought to be no class in politics, and that a working man who has equal or higher abilities ought to have as generous support from the upper classes as the gentlemen get from the lower. We are determined also that we will be consulted in every election, and have no hole-and-corner nominations by self-constituted leaders. Those are the principles I'm fighting for here; and, it strikes me, they are principles none of you will understand thoroughly until we have let a lot of Fogies slip into Parliament."

Pivot bit his lips. He was thinking what infinite idiots were the reforming busybodies who had made these awkward electoral incidents possible. They were the distraction of a party—especially of a Popular party with its confounded variety of opinions.

***

XIII.—Explosion—of a totally new Fulminating Agent.

MEANTIME a mine was preparing for Mr. Pivot of a very unexpected character. No sooner had he left Mr. Richey, than that gentleman put on his hat and went over to Mr. Heneage's committee-rooms. He was excited.

"Mr. Heneage," said he, "Lord Bantam's friends, and my Lord Haricot, and the Treasury have to-day passed an insult upon me which I venture to say is unprecedented in my family history. Read that letter [*Lord H.'s*] and that [*Tilson's*].

Heneage read and profited. He handed them to his agent whose eyes twinkled. The latter seemed to be revolving some programme or newspaper placard in his mind; for he said musingly, "Unprecedented affair—Treasury dictation in elections—extraordinary perversion of a trust for political purposes by a Ministerial peer. Mr. Richey," said he, " you have won us the election."

After half an hour's consultation, the following letter was addressed to the Prime Minister :—

TO THE RIGHT HONOURABLE UDOLPHO POLKINGHORNE, M.P.
&c., &c., &c.

Treasury, Whitehall.

SIR,

I have the honour to address you on a matter of extreme importance. A most unusual and improper interference in the freedom of election has taken place on the part of your subordinates in the Treasury, and of a Cabinet Minister of high position—of so grave a character as seriously to jeopardise the Ministry if made public.

A Treasury agent has been sent down to this borough during a contested election, for the express purpose of assisting a particular Popular candidate, though there are two others in the field; who has, without even paying me the courtesy of calling upon me, canvassed on behalf of that candidate; and has, moreover, endeavoured to use undue influence in weaning from me some of my supporters.

I cannot conceive that conduct so disingenuous and so utterly at variance with the proper management of a great party should have been adopted with your concurrence.

I have further to inform you that the Right Honourable the Lord President of the Council—who is a trustee of the estate to which the largest interest in this borough is attached—has used the fortuitous position given him by that relation, to exercise undue influence and pressure upon the tenants of that estate in favour of Lord Bantam. It is unnecessary for me to point out the damaging effect which a disclosure of this fact would have upon the prestige of the Ministry, and I appeal to you to see that such remedy is applied as may afford me complete reparation for this most injurious and improper intervention.

I have the honour to be,
Sir,
Your most obedient, humble servant,
FREDERICK COKE HENEAGE.

This letter was forwarded by train and specially delivered. It acted like a shell at the Treasury. Messengers radiated in all directions. A telegram conveyed the news to Pivot, whose quick apprehension took in the effect of the letter in a moment. This was electioneering of the highest order. By the down train arrived a Treasury messenger, with a letter to Heneage, boldly refuting all his inferences; asserting that Lord Haricot had positively declined to interfere in the election and had strictly adhered to his determination; that his letter to Pike had been simply one of courtesy (copy enclosed), and that Mr. Richey had evidently mistaken the tenour of the communication made to him.

What the Treasury communicated to Mr. Pivot he

kept to himself. But he called together Lord Bantam's inner council. A very long conference ensued. That also was secret. Mr. Simpleton there expressed himself with some animation, and protested that they ought to go on. He assured them that he had "been over the borough" and felt perfectly certain, if matters were left in his hands, that he could return his lordship. Before the daylight had closed it was whispered about the town that the young lord had retired, and the crowd that collected round the "Moon and Green Cheese" soon read the confirmation in an advertisement posted on either side of the door. Simpleton's disgust was inexpressible. He had got hold of six experienced fellows by whom he would have succeeded in convincing a large number of voters of Lord Bantam's superiority—at any price. But he confessed that these new ways of electioneering were "unsettling his stomach."

Heneage's triumph was only momentary. At the nomination Ruggles had the show of hands; at the poll the Honourable Captain Cavendishe led his opponents by nearly two hundred and fifty votes. Of these, one hundred were friends of the trades-unionist, and the other hundred and fifty were supporters of Mr. Heneage. The arguments that had transformed them were employed during the course of the night that preceded the day of polling.

***

XIV.—The Press express their Opinions.

THE *fiasco* at Woodbury afforded an opportunity to the press for some sparkling criticisms. Nearly everybody had a rap over the knuckles. Mr. Heneage was blamed for his "unjustifiable ambition," his "overweening self-confidence," his "disregard of the amenities of party discipline;" threatened with everlasting political reprobation for "dividing the party." The Ministerial journals were specially vicious. Lord Bantam's success, it was represented with great truth, would have been certain, had no other candidate appeared in the field. He was the first to offer himself, had been selected by the local heads of the party, approved by the leaders in London; and it was most unreasonable that a gentleman of comparatively unknown name without any claims upon the party, should have taken advantage of some small local discontent to organize opposition. Populars all over the country were warned that discipline was essential to party success, and reminded that free-lance politicians were parliamentary nuisances. Poor Ruggles had no mercy. His assumptions were characterised as impudent, and the fallacious nature of the claims of working men to representation were rather illogically pointed out on the one hand, while it was argued on the other that in effect there was already a fair proportion of working-men representatives in the House. Tomkins was asked why he should have interposed his vain and hopeless candidature at so critical a period, thereby distracting the attention of the electors. Amidst all these objurgations it was omitted to be observed that the object of a party organization and a parliamentary whip was to prevent such occurrences. Whether a little more tactical skill at head-quarters might not have secured a victory for the party at the expense of a disappointment to the Government was not asked, though a most pertinent question. Mr. Ruggles, in a letter to the *Chimes*, very bluntly told the Ministry that "the people cared very little about Ministries but very much about principles, and that if they attempted to dictate to free boroughs who their representatives were to be, or to use undue influences in favour of one class or quality in their own party against another, they would deserve to be defeated by the Fogies at every election until they had come to a sense of what the Popular party was, and how only it could be managed."

The reins which are to direct a party of progress must necessarily be looser than the curbs which are to hold in hand the party of obstruction. The Tartar will guide half a hundred wild and unsociable dogs in a pack, without reins, by his voice; your aristocratic whip holds in his pampered four-in-hand with double curbs and flogs them with an active lash. They are both masters in driving, and both succeed in getting out of their team the largest possible results, but their different tactics are owing to the difference in the animals.

XV.—M.P.

The annoyance caused by this failure to the Ffowlsmere family was short lived. The borough of Ffowlsmere was held by an obedient servant of the Earl, who shortly after found him an office, and thereupon Lord Bantam was returned without opposition. On presenting himself to the constituency the inveterate Broadbent formed a party to oppose him; but our hero developed a breadth of view which completely won over the Chartist leaders. He even professed many of their principles. His religion was clearly as unsettled as their own, and his Communistic views were in such strange contrast with his enormous prospects that Broadbent began to hope that this youth was to be the pioneer of a new Socialistic era. For the present the shoemaker was compelled to be satisfied with vague pledges, but he looked forward to creating in the borough a party strong enough to demand something more specific. The young lord scandalized his most respectable supporters by insisting that Broadbent should second him at the nomination—a humiliation to which it took all the weight of his wealth and position to reconcile them to submit. In this way Lord Bantam became a Member of Parliament.

* *
*

XVI.—Disaster to a Prig Ministry.

LORD BANTAM took the oaths and his seat for Ffowlsmere. At this time the state of parties in the House and the position of the Ministry were peculiar. It was suffering from a Prig incubus. Its chief—one may say its heaviest members were of that anachronistic class that appertains to the era of primary reform; an era which has almost become to the scientific student of politics a fossil period, wherein are stratified not a few monsters and other relics—in stone. The Prigs are a well-known party. They are zealous for progress—when it is least agitated. They have a Dervish-like proficiency in tergiversation. Their theories and professions are ostentatiously liberal; but in fact they are the most niggardly of political benefactors. A Prig is a Fogy without principle and a Radical without practice.

The ministry then in power was that of Mr. Polkinghorne, a Prig by birth and education. He was ably supplemented by the Earl of Ffowlsmere, Lord Haricot, and other distinguished Prigs. A few diluted Radicals taken into the Cabinet as a concession to the extremists, but rigidly selected with reference to their moderation or their known impressibility, were insufficient to infuse into this highly respectable Government the life-blood of progress. For some years peace on the Continent and prosperity at home had prolonged conditions favourable to the quiescence of this ministry. But unhappily men will think. REQUIESCAT IN PACE is only written on dead men's tombs; and Mr. Polkinghorne found that it was not to be inscribed on his administration. The people became conscious of social wants and of corresponding Government neglects, and in looking round to remedy these, found themselves obstructed by the state of the political machinery wherewith the regeneration was to be worked. The Public Health was in an unendurable state, and there was neither law nor organization to improve it. No efforts were being made to redress those inequalities between the capitalist and labourer, which must exist and increase unless the latter has some artificial aid from a power superior to both to adjust the balance. They discovered that the chronic agitations of an island attached to the empire had become so serious as to necessitate immediate legislation, and they resolved that the long-tried methods of quieting the aspirations of a people—fiery and foolish in too many things, yet having their rights before God and man—must now be displaced by measures more rational. A strong national feeling was growing in favour of the provision of education by the State, and a subordinate agitation arose out of it concerning the question of procuring the necessary schools by a concurrent endowment of denominations. The labour organizations were demanding that Government should superintend the migration of labour within the kingdom, and the emigration from it. Indeed the country had clearly resolved that it had too long rested and been thankful with exemplary patience, and it now began to yawn and stretch its arms portentously. In doing so, like Gulliver with the Lilliputians, it shook the ministry rather roughly.

As is too frequently necessary—and perhaps much too often wrongly considered necessary—the minds of the people looked towards the accomplishment of these great ends by overhauling the political machinery. A tremendous agitation shook the country, having for its aim the Reconstitution of Electoral Districts. It was represented that many small constituencies were more powerful than large ones—that glaring inequalities yet remained as a legacy from the past era of obstruction—that the effect of these inequalities was to cripple the popular vote and give undue power to the limited classes. Until this was changed, it was alleged, there could be no hope of obtaining a truly Popular House and a truly Popular ministry.

The government of Mr. Polkinghorne—pledged, so far as hustings-speeches went, to facilitate the representation of the people—found itself compelled to take up the question. It had brought in several bills in successive sessions—and had permitted them not to succeed. At length the country would brook delay no longer. Excitement ran high. Vast public meetings were held in large halls or in the open air. Immense bodies of men from six to ten abreast filed for hours before the clubs and palaces at the West-end of the metropolis, for the purpose of enabling their tenants to count the numbers of persons who disagreed with them—perhaps a not altogether useless lesson in arithmetic. Squirmingham went into hysterics, with its mayor incessantly in the chair. Cottonchester wasted its hours in spinning indignant orations. Liversedge, Ironchester, Radford, sent deputations to the Prime Minister. He, on account of their magnitude, was obliged—with the leave of the Domestic Minister, who had all obstructions carefully removed for the purpose—to receive them in the Park, and paid them extreme courtesy. The "Redistribution League," constituted by some very able artisans in London, spread its ramifications through the country. Of course the Government had been obliged to bring in a bill, and of course it was unsatisfactory. It had the flavour of Priggism. It preserved too carefully the county influence, and the very object of the Radicals was to reduce that influence to the minimum. The Fogies were dissatisfied with it because it was too Radical, and uniting with their opponents below the gangway in a division on the second reading, they, just three weeks after Lord Bantam had become a member of the House, threw out the bill and the ministry.

Our young lord, who sat below the gangway, had been eager to show that he was a Minerva legislator and needed no suckling. He spoke twice before the catastrophe—once on the question of facilitating the acquisition of homes by artisans in great cities—and the second time, on the Redistribution Bill, in a very ambitious speech against the Government, of which his father was a member. At this the Earl lost his temper, and rated him soundly for his unnatural conduct. To which he replied that his conscience had compelled him to act as he had done. Whereupon the Earl, with true Prig consistency, "d—d his conscience."

XVII.—The Claims of Society on its Gods.

Now fairly launched upon the world—Peer's son, Rotterdam heir, member of Parliament, budding statesman, author—Lord Bantam was a conspicuous object. A star like this could shine with no dim splendour. But if stars are sublunary enough to be reached by human enterprise their destiny is to do more than twinkle. The young lord had taken some quiet chambers at St. James's, expecting to be left to do his work as a people's representative.

In a few weeks the number of circulars, cards, letters, newspapers, forwarded to him from all parts of the United Kingdom, from people of every nation, sex and profession, from corporate and incorporate bodies, and from the clergy, struck him aghast. He found it necessary to hire another room and employ a secretary. He was good natured, he was energetic, he was open to flattery, he was heir to fabulous wealth. These were dangerous qualifications in England just then. So many people were anxious to take advantage of them. The number of agents who called for subscriptions to societies, philanthropic or otherwise, was legion. He went into a good deal of their work with avidity. He became Vice-President of the "Poor Authors' Society" at the usual expense of £50. He held the same office for the "Centenarian Widows' Fund" and the "Society for the Reclamation of Waste Women." He became a Patron of the "Good Samaritan Insurance Club," the only appropriateness one could distinguish in the name being that it was certain to land its client on the back of an ass.

But Lord Bantam proved of too earnest and practical a turn of mind for the managers of some of these charities. In many of them those qualities were gladly welcomed and happily utilised. Others deemed him needlessly intrusive into the conduct of their business or the state of their accounts. Thus he scandalised the managers of the Centenarian Widows' Fund, by suggesting that the annual dinner should be foregone by the subscribers and devoted to the widows, but the secretary and managers hastily explained that dinners were means to extract aid from the consumers of them. Lord Bantam was incredulous. He would not believe that the gift of any really charitable person could be given or withheld on motives so gross and trivial. But he was admittedly a novice. The officials were better acquainted with the grounds of British benevolence, and since their own living was at stake they may be taken to have been correct.

He was besieged both in and out of the House, by promoters of public companies, who set before him authentic estimates for making money without trouble. He was simply asked to "lend his name" as a director. It is a singular fact that to such allurements Lord Bantam was particularly open. Wealth never seems to oversatisfy its possessor. The insatiable MORE rules the millionnaire and the pauper alike. It was a pleasure to him to exhibit a talent for business and to increase his already exorbitant riches. The Earl his father was not disinclined to encourage him in this line, cautioning him to investigate carefully every scheme proposed to him. In the course of a year Lord Bantam's name adorned nearly twenty prospectuses of public companies, along with peers, M.P.'s, and supposititious capitalists. To any other man the results would have been ruinous. It was not until he had narrowly escaped a criminal prosecution that he had the strength to resist the tempting proposals set before him by stock-jobbing fellow-legislators in the lobbies of Parliament.

* * *

XVIII.—Nobility and the Working Man.

I AM inclined to think that at this time our hero was the prey of an ambition such as sometimes afflicts ardent minds even outside of asylums. Broadbent had thoroughly convinced himself and succeeded in persuading the young lord that "there was a great career before him." This career was to come to a glorious consummation in the transfiguration of labour and the regeneration of society. It was pointed out to Lord Bantam that, as labour must get its rights and society was sure to be regenerated, it would be no mean honour to be the leader in that illustrious movement. There is a patent vagueness in the terms employed and as much in the object, but both sounded and seemed very magnificent. To a man of such forced intellectual activities, various sympathies and supreme philosophies as Bantam, the prospect was transcendent, and the few mountains of obstruction which appeared in the way dwindled into mole-hills. The dreams of the proletariat rested upon a condition of things which I must, at the risk of being tedious, describe with a little detail.

In the political character of the British artisan there was much to discourage his most generous admirer. The influence of feudal tyranny, of debasing patronage, of a vicious system of poor relief, of reckless and inordinate charity, of an ignorance,—the peril and evil of which lay at the door of long-protracted Prig indifference, supported by Fogy inertness and clerical bigotry,—showed their cruel effects in the condition of the working-classes.

Against this state of things, how could they, poor weaklings! fight? Out of the mire of it how blindly, wildly, must they struggle! What generous sympathy and patient forbearing help did they require in their difficult efforts to enhance their position!

This was the state in which Lord Bantam found them, and, I regret to say, has left them. They had organized themselves in a rough way at first, but afterwards with remarkable success, into associations for protecting the Rights of Labour. In doing this, no wonder if they often erred, often went to extremes, often broke the conditions of the social compact; the injustice was not always on their side. They had in certain instances recognised objects of common good, and with the aid of noble men from other classes had attained them. They were still dissatisfied. They were conscious that they needed more—not always sensible or always agreed what that more was. Some looked to political change and revolution as the torch of their social improvement. Others looked to projects apparently more utilitarian and less ambitious, such as that the State should organize the labour of the country; superintend the disposition of profits, of land, of food; in fact, that the Government should be the father and mother of the nation. They did not see how impracticable such a scheme was; that the freest of governments must of necessity be the least paternal; that the best which is done for a man is what he does for himself; that the most they could ask society to do—*and that was much*—was to prompt and foster judicious measures when there was danger of their lying undone for want of such aid—to remove the impediments, legal, social, political, religious, which on nearly every hand obstructed progress and enterprise; and lastly, that though society did ignore many of its duties, remedies in the proposed degree would almost have involved its destruction.

Among these men had arisen able leaders, not always wise or discreet perhaps, some of them not always trustworthy, yet many of them men of good metal and earnest spirit. But envy, detraction, jealousy, incompatibility of view, temper, aim, religion struck wide savage gaps through the vast mass, and everywhere it yawned with divisions and lost its concrete strength. No wonder with such a mass! So terribly inert, so sadly ignorant, so corrupted by the evil negligence of the past, so deficient in the elements of political cohesion. How weeds and thorns flourished in it! How Infidels, Revolutionists, Red Communists spread their vicious contagion among the reeking millions, and how society looked on, and trembled, and wondered what the end would be—and did nothing.

Lord Bantam marking these things, thought, with hasty

and impulsive generalisation, that the end ought to be the Commune, and that he would be doing a patriot's duty in pioneering that end. He enthusiastically dedicated himself to the propagation of theories of free thought and free life. He disregarded the less lofty but equally noble and more practical possibilities of good lying at his hands: in the various measures for securing to the labourer healthier homes, better dwellings, facilities for internal and colonial transit; for opening to their energies the vast land resources of the empire and encouraging their development of them; in improving their relations with their employers; in removing all hindrances to their free association and coöperation; in extending to them the benefits of ordinary and technical education; in freeing the land from feudal restraints and superstitions, from an impolitic law of settlement, from the evils of primogeniture, from the incubus of mortmain, and from the obstructions, legal or otherwise, to its cheap and easy transfer; in reclaiming for the settlement of labourers vast tracts now lying waste; and in those thousand-and-one remedies which lie in removal of restrictions. These great measures, which society might with some safety engage in, were discarded by our hero for the extravagant and impracticable dreams of the Commune.

He naturally came under the notice of political intriguers. He subscribed to a Society for the Abolition of the Sabbath, and attended meetings held in Bellowsbury, by a brawler who combined secret plotting, open-air preaching, and organizing demonstrations on every question affecting the working-classes, with a shallow irreligion. This person made a living out of ingenious blasphemy, and procured currency for opinions not otherwise vendible, by mixing them with profanity.

Lord Bantam's ostentatious principles of general humanity led him to overlook these evil accidents, and he professed to find in this man's work a ground of good and verity which justified him in assisting it. So grossly had he mistaken Kelso's teaching. How much capacity of good he himself may have lost by his indiscreet and needless boldness he never seems to have considered, and we are not called upon to estimate.

PART VI.

HOW HE EMBRACED THE ECLECTIC RELIGION.

I.—Society—at large.

OUR hero had spent his life thus far somewhat apart from the company of the other sex. The Countess's fashionable cliques did not attract him. It was the society of a lady intriguing for a party with which he had few sympathies. The fresh young belles of the season were unknown to a young lord engaged in revolutionary politics, philosophic philanthropies and the exercise of eloquence. It was therefore not without awkwardness that he at first made his *début*. Both the Earl and Countess, hoping to wean him from his "odd views," impressed upon him the necessity of taking his place in the social intercourse of his class. Perhaps they hoped for a lucky alliance with some charming devotee of the party to disperse his youthful illusions. In acceding to their desire, he did so with bad grace. Society was anxious to see him, not only for his distinguished position, but because of his peculiarities; his red hair and notorious opinions were suggestively coupled wherever the former appeared. On the other hand, he was cool and self-confident in argument; his speech had a startling and rather rude directness; his voice even was somewhat strident. When the time came for him to dine at Lady Singleton's, and to take down the most fascinating belle of the season, the Honourable Emmeline Wycherley, who was equal to anything and anybody, from the Derby or *tableaux vivants* with those gay lords, Stableton and Guy, to a royal garden party or an Evangelical bishop, young Bantam was a mere baby in her hands. She chatted so brightly and so rapidly—with such *naïve* affectation, such sly, coy wit—the young lord did not know where he was. He had formed in his celibate and abstracted mind his own ideal of a woman —something quite different from the sparkling creature beside him; something pensive and powerful, tender yet strong, able to wrestle with, yet always submissive to his mightier nature—an angel and a Goddess of Reason. But this actual young lady played with his gravest premisses, cut short his conclusions, laughed at his most serious arguments, and dispersed with gay contumely his serried array of opinions.—

> Why she would flout the devil, and make blush
> The boldest face of man that ever man saw.
> He that hath best opinion of his wit,
> And hath his brainpan fraught with bitter jests
> (Or of his own or stolen or howsoever),
> Let him stand ne'er so high in 's own conceit,
> Her wit's a sun that melts him down like butter,
> And makes him sit at table pancake-wise,
> Flat, flat, and ne'er a word to say.

She **asked him** about the races.

He protested ignorance of the turf—well he might—and raised his eyebrows when she told him she already had several " ponies on the Oaks."

She unfolded a wide and varied intimacy with theatrical gossip, both from before and behind the scenes ; and told him how that sad fellow, Lord Herrick, was quite infatuated with the celebrated Bella. The celebrated Bella was unknown to Lord Bantam, and he said so. The beauty affected to raise *her* eyebrows this time.

She then gave him a lively account of her brother's election for Wrongwich, when she canvassed a whole district for him ; how she and her mamma helped him to floor his opponent, a military officer, by an earnest crusade against the Outrageous Distempers Bill. Had he ever gone into that question ? Did he know, her mamma and she were members of a committee for agitating against the bill ? Lord Bantam blushed most foolishly, and owned that he had never examined the literature of that subject. Very well ; she would be sure and tell mamma to send him a package of the pamphlets : every one was interested in the matter now, and she herself had made two colonels promise to vote against it in the House. She hoped he would be converted, and would help them.

By the way, talking of that bill, her friend, her dearest friend, Sophronia Enequil,—daughter of the Earl of Chepstowe you know,—was one of those who had come forward to engage publicly in the crusade against the bill. She always was a blue-stocking, and indeed every one admitted she was very clever. Her speeches and essays were getting to be quite celebrated. Had he read "Woman and her Master, or the Tables Turned"?

This work had escaped his observation.

Sophronia was connected also with the "Society for Developing the Mental and Moral Stamina of Woman," —in fact, was its honorary secretary.

Bantam admitted that this was a new phase of sociology to him, and promised to study it.

Had he heard the new Dean? All the world was going to hear him. His sermons were so touching and so graceful, with so much thought, and such a manner. It quite thrilled one, and made one cry sometimes. Besides, the Dean was always preaching to statesmen, and she understood Lord Bantam was really expected to be a very distinguished statesman—a sly compliment which brought down the colour from his hair into his cheeks.

When the gentlemen rejoined the ladies in the drawing-room, Bantam found himself insensibly attracted to the side of the vexatious charmer. She was placing a new photograph in her album. It was that of an exquisitely pensive face, with such finely moulded features, such ripe, sweet lips, such a Grecian chin, and over what seemed to be magnificently lustrous eyes, such long bewitching lashes. Ignorant as he was of the *demi-monde*, he recognised it instantly as one, common enough in fast men's rooms at the University, of a woman whose name was notorious in every mouth; and looking at it aghast, he rather hastily stayed the young lady's hand as she was slipping the card into the book.

"You are very rude," said she, half playfully and half in earnest.

"I—I—I beg your pardon," said Lord Bantam in some confusion. "I was struck by the likeness; and I thought—in fact, I know whose portrait this is, and I was sure you did not. Perhaps, if you knew, you might not like to have it among the faces of your friends."

"Oh," replied Miss Wycherley, laughing, as she completed the setting, "you must not go about giving moral lectures in society. I know who it is perfectly well. I have seen her often enough in the Park, with Lord Guy. It is Nora Day. He told me her story, and her face is very charming. I don't mind who the person is, so long as the face is pretty."

He silently looked over the pages, and again and again detected faces and forms of dubious French aspect, alongside of Her Majesty, Her Majesty's daughters, the beautiful Princess of Wales, the Honourable Miss Wycherley's most cherished lady-friends, her dearest relations; and conceitedly resolving in his own mind that *his* likeness should never be seen in that singular galaxy, rather abruptly took his leave.

"Heigho!" cried Miss Wycherley to her mamma, "Lord Bantam is a philosophical fop, without manners, who at twenty-one" (she was just nineteen) " assumes to give the cue for morals to the rest of society. *A bas les despotes!"*

"Emmeline," replied her ladyship cautiously, "he will be the richest man in England."

When virtue speaks with the lips of the richest man in England, she is entitled to be despotic, and vanity may well hold her tongue.

The Honourable Miss Wycherley's conversation, trivial as it seems, did not speedily pass from the young lord's memory. He kept his promise to study the question of the subjection of women—a study for which already ample literature was provided. His facile mind soon seized upon the points, and he regarded them with favour. At the Radical Club he met with an advanced philosopher of high literary standing, who set before him the correct theses of the new school.

So rapidly do convictions change and grow in this tropical era—especially amongst ambitious statesmen!—it was not many months before our young lord could have viewed with resignation almost any pretensions put forward by what he had hitherto regarded as the weaker sex.

* *

II.—Developing the Mental and Moral Stamina of Woman.

In the time of his newly budding enthusiasm, Lord Bantam came into contact with the Society for Developing the Mental and Moral Stamina of Woman. His connection with it exercised an important influence on his future life. The Countess of Ffowlsmere had been for a short time a patroness of this institution and had attended its meetings. In the incipient stages it was a mild form of blue-stocking fever. In fact it was a literary club, where what are termed strong-minded views were entertained—that term I presume being relative to the persons concerned. At the meetings everything was discussed that did not immediately and properly relate to woman and her duties in life—duties most of which are prescribed by nature with vexatious rigidity. One of the most annoying facts the ladies had to meet was, that although a woman might refuse to take into her hands so paltry yet useful a thing as a needle, she could hardly avoid the obligation of nursing were she a mother. There are clearly matters in which woman's "sphere" is peculiar. But the good ladies of this society ignored these impertinent facts, and confined themselves to negativing masculine superiority—a field as safe as any polemical field could be. I ought to mention that the clique from its outset was of a democratic character. On the committee Peeresses and Honourable Mesdames and Misses sat side by side with authoresses and milliners and governesses, and the meetings were of very composite material.

For awhile the discussions and publications of this society were more dry than startling. The unexceptionable subjects of the right of females to vote, of protection to married women's property, of the higher education of women, were treated, if with no novelty, with great propriety. Gentlemen were occasionally admitted to learn wisdom from the new reformers. The Earl of Ffowlsmere had presided at one meeting; even Lord Evergood had taken the chair at another; but, on the whole, the males distinguished by this privilege were philosophers, men of a meek spirit and selected for that qualification. They never lifted up their voices in any but the mildest applause or deprecation.

But, the society increasing, a new element began to develop itself. Several very vigorous ladies were introduced. Mrs. and the Misses Croquet, Lady Sophronia Enequil, the Hon. Flora Temperley, Miss Virginia Crabb who had adopted the Positivist philosophy, Mrs. Dart, writer of three-volume novels which just skimmed the edge of Lord Campbell's Act, Miss Debrett, authoress of social articles in a sensational magazine, and other ladies whose antecedents were unknown, had no sooner joined the institute, than they began to give a boldness and liveliness to the discussions which disconcerted some of the elders. Many of the latter withdrew, among them Lady Ffowlsmere. The effect of this withdrawal was to give fresh notoriety to the association, and to increase its membership from that class of floating women of independent means, strong minds and no husbands, who occasionally emerge and distract society. The institution now became largely leavened with a real masculine element. It was at this time that Lord Bantam was invited to take the chair at one of its meetings. He had expatiated on the "Sphere of Woman," in the Literary Coliseum, a review which had space for a hundred thousand opinions. A letter, written in a masculine hand, from the Honorary Secretary Lady Sophronia Enequil, invited him to preside at a meeting of the society, when she was to read a paper on "Comte's Estimate of the Feminine." His mother informed him that Lady Sophronia, daughter of the Earl of Chepstowe, was a young lady of brilliant talents and an original character.

"I must warn you," said the Countess, "that the association is now a very queer one—but then you like queer things. I understand they have grown quite shocking, and that the most absurd theories are advanced. The last I heard of was a motion that marriage ought to be made a matter of contract terminating from year to year; a suggestion which, apart from its obvious inconveniences, is so atrociously immoral, that in my opinion its propagation should be suppressed by law. Sophronia is a lady with all her peculiarities, and very clever and engaging, so I would have you beware of her, if you must go and preside over such strange conclaves."

Bantam accepted the honour with pleasure. For a whole morning he dipped into the "Philosophie Positive" to refresh his memory and glean some idea of the doctrines to be propounded by the fair essayist. In the evening he drove to the hall where the intellectual orgies of advanced femininity were held. Ladies were descending from cabs at the door. Others were coming alone and on foot. His Lordship began to think that he *was* going into a "queer" place. He was received by three ladies in bonnets, and two destitute of those accidents, who exhibited short-cut curly hair, and wore unusually limited skirts. The Committee. A solitary gentleman grinned to him a welcome. This was a little man with an excessively small head, small eyes, nose slightly *retroussé*, mouth large and full of teeth, which were always glistening. His tall thin neck stood up between huge shirt collars. He was dressed in rather seedy black—a professional gentleman. Not a clergyman—perhaps a surgeon. It turned out he was a school-teacher and a Unitarian minister. His name was Chatters. There often seems to be a special providence in the assignment of names.

But the prominent person to Lord Bantam's eye was the honorary secretary, Lady Sophronia. She was not handsome, nor could it be said that she was the reverse. Her face was a face of thought, perhaps of power, certainly of determination—with flashing uneasiness in the brown eyes. *The* feature of features was her nose. If it were it not quite so formidable as the tower of Lebanon looking towards Damascus, it stood forth a prominent beacon to all beholders. Its proportions overawed the rest of her face. It discountenanced the most impertinent boldness in an observer. With that nose before him, the spectator found it impossible to be frivolous or to assume an air of patronage. On the contrary, it was so potential, you felt it must have its way. You would have stepped into the gutter to avoid its onset. Perhaps the full mouth and lips, and the fine teeth when they were shown, as they were when she was animated, did to some extent mitigate the tyrannical attitude of that nose, but it was only mitigation. When Lord Bantam came under the shadow of it he succumbed to its influence. Lady Sophronia took him in hand and did what she liked with him. She explained to him what line she intended to take, and what she wished him to say. He was not sure whether he agreed with it, whether it was rational or logical, but he was incapable of objection. It was a case of nasal duress.

They entered the hall, which was pretty well filled. It could be seen at a glance that a number of fashionables had been attracted by the programme, among whom were not a few young ladies of immature years. There also appeared to be numbers of male and female nondescripts.

The young Lord sat scratching his red hair in search of ideas. Lady Flora Temperley moved that he take the chair. He took it, and rose to speak amid treble cheers. The ladies affected parliamentary usages. He said:

"Ladies and Gentlemen—or perhaps as a testimony to my acknowledgment of equality I ought to say—'my friends,' irrespective of sex (cheers), I cannot easily express how flattered I am at the honour conferred upon me in asking me to preside at a meeting so important, so peculiar. Time was when such an assemblage for such a purpose was impossible. Anterior to creation (laughter) —do not misunderstand me—anterior, I say, to creation, if there ever was one, there must have existed in a creative mind the Idea of that human nature which has through rising ages developed into two seemingly diverse if not antagonistic lines which we denominate the sexes. Modern science, ranging the universe in search of truth, and working with a diligence and accuracy previously unknown, has ascertained with certainty that that primordial Ideal was not double but duplex (cheers)— that it was in fact duality in unity—it was that which now we never see except in plants and some of the lower species of the animal kingdom—hermaphroditical perfection (cheers). Nay, there is ground to believe, that the original of us all, in the simious shape, was such a perfect dual unity: and although now undoubtedly in our human development, preponderance is given to one or other of its antecedent accidents, we know with precision that it is a matter of the merest chance, and I may add of the most indifferent moment, whether of these two possible accidents shall be in the ascendant. I say 'accidents,' because science has now informed us, that the difference between what are called the sexes is not matter of substance (cheers), it is purely matter of form. How illogical then is it that mankind should for ages have drawn and observed distinctions neither justified nor intended in the primary Ideal! Our great naturalist has by his researches in the physical world proved this fact—and no doubt had the distinguished French philosopher whose ideas are destined to regenerate mankind and transform the aspects of society (cheers), only had the advantage of the more recent scientific discoveries, his views on the position of women would have been seriously modified. Surely the positivism of Comte must lead us to the same conclusion with the speculations of Darwin. Man is everywhere man. In the eye of a divine philosophy, of a correct science, man and woman are unknown—all is man (cheers). This is the truth so important in its bearing upon social relations and social conditions that no doubt with convincing logic and brilliant rhetoric, the fair essayist (murmurs)—I beg pardon, the learned secretary (cheers)—will develop for us this evening from her study of Comte. I beg to call on Lady Sophronia Enequil to read her paper."

With this masterly speech I must pray the reader to be satisfied. I should much prefer not reporting all that the honorary secretary said, for she pursued the lines she had indicated to the Chairman with a frankness as embarrassing to report as it was startling to hear. The great Comte would himself, though a Frenchman, have gone mad on the spot had he listened to half the extraordinary things said upon his text.

When the applause that succeeded to the reading of the essay had subsided, Mrs. Fullalove, a lady with a far from unpleasing tendency to manliness both in her frame and mode of thought, made a clever speech. She pointed out how unjustly woman was treated under the existing "masculine régime." She declared that the selfishness and jealousy of mankind shut out her sex from fields of occupation in which they would shine with surpassing splendour. She declared that deficiences of education alone prevented woman from taking her stand side by side with her "male correlative" in science, in philosophy, in politics and medicine. She instanced the term "Husband" or "*House-bond*," as indicative of the fact that in an earlier and more natural age—of course she rejected the foolish and fabulous history called Scripture—the family father was not looked upon as the dictator, but as the "*nexus* of the coëqual elements of the family." "Now," she added, "to modern wives, this tie ought to be designated house-bondage—the nexus has become a knout, &c." Mrs. Fullalove always deserves to be commended for the moderation of her remarks.

Mr. Chatters, in his anxiety to unsex himself, went much further. He declared the anomalies of sexual relations to be due to the unnatural superstitions that obtained in society on the subject of marriage. He asserted that large families tended to the degradation of woman, since they involved on her part the sacrifice of freedom and placed her in a position of which men could take advantage to keep her in subjection. He said that the French had, with the quick apprehension and philosophic acumen peculiar to that nation, detected this circumstance, and had been gradually, by their admirable system, reducing marriage to its proper status. He said other things, at which not a few ladies concealed their faces.

Would you believe it? No sooner had the delicate subject last alluded to been thus broached by this brazen and shallow prattler, than a number of females seized upon it with avidity. Even the noble Chairman began to find it uncomfortable, and he occasionally called the most refractory to order, but quite enough escaped to testify that the institute had become a very advanced school indeed. When a woman once oversteps the bounds of prudery, unless, as is sometimes the case, she is an Angel with a special mission from heaven, there is no telling what range she will take, and society may be forgiven if it looks with concern upon a movement which seems to incur even a chance that such assemblies or such ideas should become familiar to the wives and daughters of England.

III.—The Eclectic Religion.

"Mamma," said Lord Bantam, not many mornings after the incident related in the previous chapter, "I was very much interested in Lady Sophronia the other evening. She is somewhat transcendental for a Positivist, but her mind is powerful and her eloquence somewhat remarkable."

"Very," said the wary Countess, feeling her way; "but did you not notice a strange want of feeling—of delicacy—or rather, I should say, of sensibility?"

"On the contrary," replied Bantam, slightly colouring; "I gathered, of course only from a very slight notice, that her strength of intellect is very much invigorated by passion. You could see she is quite an enthusiast—but she tempers it admirably."

"I hope," said the Countess, in some alarm, "she has touched no chord in you but that of admiration. She strikes me as the reverse of temperate; and her enthusiasm, as you term it, seems to me to be extravagance. She is not fitted for society — she openly disavows it. I never saw her at a ball in my life. Besides, compared with your own, her position is a very indifferent one."

"Oh!" said the provoking young man, "my dear mamma, a woman is always expecting a love affair. I should be afraid to give my affections to this young lady

—she is infinitely above them. She should marry a philosopher."

"I sincerely hope she may," rejoined her Ladyship. "She is certainly unfit for any ordinary being."

"Nevertheless I should think her society is worth cultivating. I suppose," said he in an insinuating tone, "she would come to a dinner party, would she not?"

The Countess with bad grace admitted that Sophronia did patronize dinner parties, and politically promised to invite her to her next literary symposium.

Among the guests invited at the same time were the Bishop of Dunshire, Lady Singleton and Miss Wycherley, and Mr. Kelso, now rising into position as a historical writer of remarkable originality and power. Kelso had been watching his pupil's course with some anxiety, the more that the latter had not of late honoured him with his confidence. The tutor somewhat reproached himself with having too frankly expressed to the young man the results of his extensive acquisitions and careful thought before a sufficient groundwork of knowledge had been laid to sustain the weight. Nothing could have been farther from his intentions than to create an incredulous Positivist Chartist Socialist Atheist out of his young charge. He saw too late that all this came of one single error. In defiance of the Pauline maxim, strong meat had been given to a babe.

The young Lord had the pleasure of sitting between

the Hon. Miss Wycherley, whom he escorted to dinner, and Lady Sophronia. The young ladies though so strangely unlike each other were very friendly. Miss Wycherley bantered her "learned friend" for deserting the "awfully jolly parties" that were going on, and asked her the title of her last article in the Coliseum.

She replied that she was then engaged on one upon the "Eclectic Religion."

The answer caused the Bishop to prick up his ears, and the Earl intervened.

"So, Lady Sophronia, you are going to discuss the new heresy? It is a tremendously wide one—seeing that it stretches over so many centuries, ages and varieties of thought."

"The latest folly," said the Bishop, "alleged to be based on scientific certainties, and yet its elementary generalisations are incorrect. A religion which ignores faith as an element of religion is a patent confutation of itself."

"That," said Lady Sophronia, "is an awkward way of putting it, no doubt; but what is religion and what is faith? Is not the latter mere sentiment unworthy of scientific observation—and is not religion a practical recognition of scientific facts in their relation to the Divine?"

The Bishop and Kelso both contended that this definition was vague and unsatisfactory.

"But," inquired Lord Bantam, to whom this subject

was a fresh one, "may I ask, what is the Eclectic Religion?"

"The Eclectic Religion," replied the Bishop, "is the negativing of every fact and principle on which faith in God and Christ and the Church rests. It is the ignoring of the Divine."

"The Eclectic Religion," said Lady Sophronia, "is the sum and substance of the true in all religions. It is the new light breaking in upon the old night. It is the destruction of idols—of superstitions—of bigots. It is formulating human experience into a divine theory. It is the grand truth that man and man only, from age to age expanding in wisdom and power is the true divinity."

Bantam was enchanted. The Countess was horrified.

"The Eclectic Religion," interposed Kelso gravely, "is an attempt to organize human ignorance into a system."

Lady Sophronia looked at the speaker, but changed the conversation.

When the company had gone the Earl said maliciously to his son, who was retiring to his lodgings:

"I wish to give you a piece of advice. Never marry a woman with a long nose. Possibly she may love you, but as you are a man, she will rule you, or you will have cause to rue her."

  * * * * * *

When the young Lord returned to his rooms, he somewhat abstractedly permitted his valet to perform his usual offices, and having been wrapped in his dressing-gown, dismissed him.

He felt himself to be under an influence equally novel and provoking. His fiery hair seemed in flames. His ears still tingled with his father's words. For some reason they had pained him. He asked himself *Why?* The answer came before him in a vision of Lady Sophronia's face with its majesty, its intellectual power, its flashing liveliness—and its dominating nose. Through his mind passed and repassed the words, "*Never marry a woman with a long nose. She will rule you, or you will have cause to rue her.*"

He said, " I couldn't think of marrying such a woman. My father's caution is a very wise one. The Duke of Wellington was a tyrant. Moreover long noses are deformities. And they descend in families. Lady Sophronia's nose is not so *very* long though. This Eclectic Religion is a very interesting subject. I was struck by her comprehensive grasp of it. I should like to call upon her to-morrow and talk about it. I must really get the Earl to define the length of nose at which danger begins, and to construct a diagram of degrees—"

*　　*　　*　　*　　*　　*

The youthful legislator retired to bed, but not to sleep. The still voices of the night seemed to whisper the name Sophronia. Ends, peaks, promontories, curves of noses, projected from cornices, beyond posts and through curtains. When at length he fell into a troubled doze, the Earl appeared before him, holding in one hand a Sheffield razor, and in the other—oh, horror! whereat he awoke—between thumb and finger the Lady Sophronia's nose.

IV.—Eclecticism in Raptures.

The ardent hair and temperament of our hero strangely affected his action at this critical period. A day and a night of inflammatory thought succeeded the evening of his first social introduction to Lady Sophronia. He was no adept at gallantry, and he instinctively shrank from confessing to the Countess a liking which to her would seem so absurd—or to the Earl a passion involving such a contempt of his nasal theory. The singularly retired habits of the young lord put it out of the question that he should have a friend capable for such an emergency. The heir of a regal estate was thrown back upon himself.

It will have been gathered that our hero was peculiarly matter-of-fact. No sooner had he ascertained by a correct analysis of his feelings that he was a subject of that emotion termed love, than he resolved that true philosophy dictated the conveyance of the information to the object of it in the shortest possible time and by the directest method. He determined to visit the Lady Sophronia at her father's house in South Dawdley Street, and arrived upon the doorstep at the unseasonable hour of ten in the morning.

The young lady's peculiarities were fostered or at least endured by her parents. She was accordingly allowed privileges not usually afforded to unmarried virgins in society. The numerous "movements" in which she was interested required that she should be approachable by a curious variety of people, so a butler's room at the side of the hall, about eight feet square, was withdrawn from menial occupation and dedicated to her morning receptions and social labours. Here, with a few books, many papers, a Davenport, an easy-chair, a stool, and a small ottoman, she might be found from ten to one every morning, habited in a short velveteen petticoat, a cloth jacket, apparently cut on the plan of a gentleman's dress-coat, and very plain collar and cuffs.

When the footman at South Dawdley Street first opened the door to our hero on the steps, with his red hair and indifferent stature, he clearly mistook him; for he said—

"If you were come to cut her ladyship's corns, she will see you in her boodwoir, if you please."

The youth's philosophy was extremely tested by this seeming reference to the fallibility of Sophronia's earthly footing, but he had his revenge on the flunky. That person's confusion was complete when he received the card of the heir to the wealthiest of British earldoms, and "umbly begging his lordship's pardon," and explaining that a "chir-roppody gentleman" was every moment expected to wait upon his young mistress, he led the way to the morning drawing-room.

"I beg pardon, my lord; was it the Countess or my young lady, my lord?"

"Oh! Lady Sophronia, if she is at home and disengaged."

The lacquey delivered the card to the young lady, suggestively informing her that Lord Bantam was in the drawing-room. She coloured faintly, and after a moment's hesitation ordered the footman to show the visitor into her room—an order that for the three-hundredth time confirmed that astounded individual of her madness. The struggle in her mind had been between her early education and her new principles. The former would have dictated mamma and the drawing-room; the latter prompted her independent self and her boudoir.

With her heightened colour, when he found himself sitting within the narrow walls of her sanctum, Lord Bantam thought Sophronia absolutely handsome; and so she was. She said—

"I have been so amused this morning in recalling the conversation of last night. I think Mr. Kelso's definition of the Eclectic Religion was so clever and yet so unjust."

"I have come," said Bantam, passing his hand through

his tawny locks, "to sit as a disciple at the feet of so fair a prophetess."

"No compliments, I pray you, Lord Bantam: I detest them."

"I sincerely ask your forgiveness. I very much want to hear more of this new religion, and to hear of it from *you*," said our hero, getting up, leaning his elbow on the high window-sill and looking Sophronia straight in the face. He was distant from her about two feet, and glanced down upon her—the light falling over her brown hair, shining into her clear eyes, and glorifying her majestic nose.

"How shall I begin?" she said quite unaffectedly; "for I am unaware how much you know, and what foundation you may have in the principles on which Eclecticism rests. Have you any acquaintance with the maxims of Confucius; or the Veda of the Rig; or the Tripitaka of the Buddha; or the Zendavesta of Zoroaster, or Emerson's Essays? I know you are intimate with the philosophy of Comte. In these we find the propositions on which have been raised the superstructure of Eclectic truth."

"No," said Bantam; "I have seen but two of these. I wish I could study them under your guidance."

He looked at her again, very hard.

"Oh!" cried she, laughing, "I am but a poor scholar—I should make a worse teacher. But I can tell you the substance of the views which Eclectics hold. We begin by eliminating from our apprehensions the idea of the Divine. This as an objective and distinct reality we negative. We insist that as it must have originated with ourselves, it is in ourselves; and that to seek for the extravagant conceptions of the personate Divine entertained by religious and Bible enthusiasts is to seek for the theoretic eidôlon of perverted fancy."

"There is no difficulty," sighed the infatuated Bantam, "in accepting the doctrine that the divine is in you. But I fear that divinity is likely to be to many enthusiasts a real eidôlon—an object of worship."

The young lady arose. She did not seem angry, but moved. She looked anxiously at the face now on a level with her own and so close to it. Her cheek was glowing; her lips, slightly apart, showed the fine pearls within; and her bosom heaved with singular and unphilosophic emotion. Lord Bantam was equally enfevered. He said—

"Sophronia—philosophy knows no titles and is fettered by no ceremonies,—I love you. You are my divinity. I accept your new gospel: I beseech you, be my teacher——"

Sophronia hastily put her hand on his lips; it was glowing with heat.

"Electicism," she said, "is modest and claims no preeminence. If, Albert, you are sincere in desiring me to tread with you the crystalline ladder to the highest wisdom, my soul is yours and yours is mine."

Lord Bantam in a moment clasped with his arm the

waist of his enthusiastic companion, and in embracing Sophronia embraced the Eclectic religion.

※ ※
※

V.—By Civil Contract.

THE infamous chiropodist interrupted the raptures of the young philosophers and restored them once more to common life and common sense. With such rapidity had they passed from sentiment to avowal that they awoke somewhat awkwardly to what was before them. They parted with a promise to meet on the morrow.

The next morning at ten Lord Bantam again stood on the door-step in South Dawdley Street. Lord and Lady Chepstowe were happily late risers, and two clear hours were before the lovers. The lacquey this time ushered his lordship directly into the literary closet of his young mistress, who received her disciple-lover with joyous fervour.

Their conference resulted in a determination to acquaint their parents at once with what had happened.

"We must," said Sophronia, "however unwillingly, pay some regard to the prejudices of the world. To us this tie needs no further confirmation either legal or parental. True souls are interwoven by transcendental bonds."

"Yes, my Sophronia," rejoined Bantam, rather passionately for a novice in amours, "the divine exolution of divine souls intertwining, surely this is of itself the bond, the æsthetic cohesion, the real and glorious marriage of a divine philosophy."

Thereupon they kissed each other very warmly for those who would seem to be content with divine exolution and an æsthetic cohesion.

Sophronia however raised a difficulty.

"My Albert," said the languishing sophist, "we must needs marry as becomes disciples of the Eclectic religion. By that ceremonies are regarded as superstitions—marriage is but an accident of sense—therefore we cannot consent to be united by those degrading and sensual rites which the Fetishist religions affect."

"No," said her lover, "we must not bend our necks to the yoke of forms. Marriage is with us a pure spiritual bond—yet it is desirable for social purposes to embody it in a contract. Let us be married by the registrar."

"We will," she replied, "without pomp or ceremony. Let it be at once. Let us delay no longer."

Lord Bantam luckily bethought him that, though it was only eleven o'clock, instantaneous marriages were by the law of England impracticable, and they curbed their impatience. He departed to the difficult task of apprising his parents of the event. Lady Sophronia's part was easy. Her communication was naturally received with the greatest satisfaction. She had out of season made the happiest hit of the season.

The young lord first disclosed his position to the Earl, who received the announcement with cold disdain.

"So you, with the finest prospects in England, have selected for your wife a blue-stocking, a visionary, an atheist. I wish you joy, sir. I cannot affect your fortune," added the old peer in a tone that denoted what he might have done had he been able; "but I shall not in the least be surprised if, after all, this step should cure you of your absurd and impulsive extremism, and ultimately convert you into a rank Fogy. As you have made your choice and are self-willed enough to insist upon it, your mother and I will keep our opinion to ourselves. We must behave to Lord and Lady Chepstowe and the young lady with the cordiality proper to their position and ours. We shall treat the affair as if it were the most acceptable match in the world."

This high-bred resolution considerably affected Lord Bantam. But he had something still more unpalatable to communicate.

"My dear father," he said with tears in his eyes, "I am overcome by your goodness. I cannot express my gratitude. The affair, as you term it, need create no unpleasantness. It will be very private. I have adopted with Sophronia the Eclectic religion. It is of course inconsistent with the pure spiritual principles of that philosophy to submit to any religious or quasi-religious ceremony. But we must enter into a legal contract——"

"Oh! you yield as much as that?" said the Earl with

a malicious smile. "I wonder your 'philosophy' would admit of anything so common-place. Perhaps you wish to be married before the registrar?"

"We do."

"Then you had better be off and get it done when you like, without further preliminary. Neither your mother nor myself can be consenting parties to such a godless business. We shall prefer to know nothing about it. Here is a cheque for a thousand pounds; and if there is to be any settlement—perhaps you will do without that, eh?—go to Messrs. Hawke and Peckham. Pray do us the favour to acquaint us of your marriage when it is consummated."

The Countess received the announcement less calmly than the Earl, but her resentment was not so deep. She fell in with her husband's policy, and even went beyond it. Lord and Lady Chepstowe had no reason to think that the union was other than welcome to the noble pair.

The wedding was never believed in by the servants of either family. Lord Bantam drove up to the bride's house in a single brougham. The bride, arrayed in a travelling costume, bade her parents an affectionate adieu and entered the carriage. They did not reappear in London for several months. The only evidence the world had of their marriage was the announcement in the newspapers. As for the gossip—imagine it!

∗

VI.—An Eclectic Symposium.

On their return to the metropolis after an extended Continental tour, Lord and Lady Bantam took a house in Belgravia, where they devoted themselves to politics, literature, social science and the Eclectic religion. We may hereafter have occasion to review some incidents of the young lord's political life; meanwhile I propose to follow him to other arenas. Lady Bantam developed into a notorious agitator. She spoke in various parts of the country against the bill for suppressing outrageous distempers by police outrages. She affected the philosophico-radical rabies against the large families of the Ginxes of society, and emphatically supported the French system. She lectured on the " prerogatives " of women, whom she affirmed to have lived under an injustice of so lengthy a period as six thousand years. In fact, the newspapers had enough to do to chronicle and write articles upon Lady Bantam's versatile activities.

The Eclectic religion had lately begun to look up in the world. Originally confined to a select and self-elected committee for the universe on behalf of truth, it had begun to extend its propagandism. Several philosophers, a number of men of science and letters, some deposed clergymen, and a few hard-headed persons of no particular employment had formed an association of Eclectic evangelists. They held meetings in various parts of the metropolis. These were called *ecclesiæ*. It was said the worship was positive; but it would have been more correct to have called it negative, since all the elements of worship were wanting. One cannot more graphically illustrate the character of these synagogues than by describing the great annual meeting of the sect at its central station, the Aryan Hall, where its Sunday worship was wont to be held. The meeting was declared by its promoters to be of a religious character.

No expense was spared to give *éclat* to this act of worship. The large hall had been cleared of its seats. In its proper balcony was stationed a fine brass band. At one end of the room various scientific curiosities were exhibited, above them a statue of Pallas. At the other a collection of ancient manuscripts and some specimens of the Sutras attracted the attention of the curious. Over these was a bust of Liberty. Round the walls were hung pictures of the "great of all ages." Among these were Socrates, Plato, Homer, Cæsar, Virgil, Lucretius, Dante, Comte, Voltaire, Mahomet, Darwin, and Dixon. Rings of immortelles hung below the frames, and white cloth amply festooned around the room gave it the aspect of a hearse for a Brobdignagian infant's funeral. Each guest was presented at the door with a laurel-wreath—emblem of his immortal humanity. When the rooms began to fill up, the effect of this distribution of green crowns was peculiar. Lady Sophronia had dressed herself in the character of Sibyl, that is to say she had framed a modern costume suggestive of that mythic and natural person. Others appeared in various philosophic costumes. The Eclectics, however, carried out their principles in their dress: it varied with the tastes of the wearers.

The "Grand Eclectic Symposium" was intended to be the latest and most perfect manifestation of enlightened humanity. It was, in the language of the school, "to be the highest evolution of the spiritual element, the physical basis, positive science, æsthetic art, the literary sublime; and finally the utmost refinement of amusement to the purposes of religion." The Programme was unique, and deserves to be reproduced in fac-simile. (See opposite page.)

The sonnet contained the following lines:—

> "Not seen, unfelt, and yet how felt and seen!
> O thou unpractical, impenetrable What!
> We cast with lightened hearts our dubious lot
>   In the dread urn—the elemental bean!
>
> "Great All, great Every, highest of Sublime;
> Inverted, introverted, controverted ONE,
> Nature's panergon, hyper-static Sun!
>   All hail in this our Syncretistic rhyme!"

As Lord and Lady Bantam were affably circulating amongst the mixed crowd after one of the dances, they encountered three gentlemen, two of whom he immediately recognised. They were Kelso and Dr. Dulcis the preacher of Woodbury. The third, a grizzly man of

GRAND ECLECTIC SYMPOSIUM AND ÆSTHETIC SOIREE.

PROGRAMME.

Opening Chorus.

The Universal Prayer . *Pope* . Music by an Amateur.

Address by the Noble the President.

On the Invalidity of the Arguments in favour of Objective Divinity.

Quadrille.

Orphée aux enfers . . . Arranged by Mr. BELSHAZZAR.

Lecture.

The Hippocampus Major and its relation to the Mosaic Cosmogony . } By Prof. CRUXLEY, F.R.S.

Song.

" Foot it featly here and there " . . By Mrs. DE TERMINY.

Valse.

Mephistophilienne . . *Faust.*

Address.

The Idolism of Tradition, or the Irrational in Sexual Probabilities . . } By Prof. MACMANUS, F.R.S., F.G.S., F.L.S.

Polka.

Der Freyschütz . . . Arranged by V. NOVELLO.

A LUCID INTERVAL.

Refreshment.

Menu.

Huitres à Voltaire.	Filets des enfans humains, Choisis au naturel par M. le Prof. DARWIN.
Saumon à Tartare.	
Petites écrevisses renversées.	Rosbif protoplastique.
Féves Pythagoriennes.	Oignons brûlés éclectiques.
Choux positifs.	Compotes de Corinthe.
Dindon fanfaronné.	Soufflés idéalogiques.
Poulets froids à l'école des philosophes.	Pâtés de *foi* gras.

Address.

Protoplastic Chaos; or the Antecedents of Life and Order . . . . . } By Lady BANTAM.

Galop.

John Brown's soul marching on . . . By A SHAKER.

Lucretian Epilogue.

God and Gammon . . . By the Rev. INFELIX NOISY, B.A.

Finale.

Benedictus Sonnet . . . By a Distinguished American.

enormous head, was presented by Kelso, and turned out to be the prophet of the times—an English Jeremiah. Bantam received Dr. Dulcis with great cordiality, and learned for the first time that he had come to reside in the metropolis. The engaging divine won Sophronia's goodwill at once. In a few minutes she was walking about the room leaning on his arm.

"I have heard of you, Dr. Dulcis," she said, "as one of the most liberal of sectarians. I however hardly venture to hope that you are here to-night as a witness of your adhesion to our faith?"

"Scarcely," said the other, smiling. "I am here to observe what the worship of this new religion is. I think no phase of human thought or devotion unworthy of study in the calmest and most liberal spirit."

"There is a touch of Eclecticism in that sentiment," said Sophronia. "May I ask what you have gathered this evening?"

"I should scarcely like upon so brief an examination," said the polished doctor, "to venture an opinion. I cannot judge how many of these people about us are in earnest. I cannot ascertain as yet what, if so, they are in earnest about. It is perhaps the narrowness of my education—but I find it impossible to conceive of worship without a Deity."

"Ah!" cried Sophronia, "my dear doctor, that is one of the fatal fallacies of all human superstition."

It will be admitted that the Christian Doctor was

more courteous than the Eclectic lady. However, they did not fall out.

Meanwhile Lord Bantam, Kelso and the Prophet had been comparing notes. From the latter his lordship received scant courtesy. He had rather flippantly asked the old Philosopher, "What he thought of this?"

"That's nothing," said the Prophet; "the question is, *What must the Great Almighty God of Israel think of this?* This to be the Religion of the Future!! This a Religion of Science? Idols of fancy hewn out of the history of the great living rocks and stones which He hath made and scattered over the wide Earth to show his Power! A 'new religion,' quotha! 'Eclectic Church?' Something better than Abraham's God—Israel's hope and helper.—David's strength—Isaiah's Anointed One! Yea, Christ Himself left in the background of the Ages by a boy lord, half a dozen tradesmen, three or four clever professors, and some dozens of women of masculine pretensions—God save us! How He must laugh!—He that sitteth in the Heavens—how his sad, terrific cacchination must ring and re-echo through the Eternal welkin as He watches the Punchinello fantastics of his little creatures here below!"

* *
*

PART VII.

HOW HE COQUETTED WITH THE PROLETARIAT.

I.—Practical Antidotes of Philosophic Theories.

WE are here compelled in four or five seconds to pass over a period of as many years in the history of our hero and his Eclectic spouse. The young Lord during that time had, under circumstances to be presently explained, continued to represent Ffowlsmere. Sophronia on her part recorded several instances of apostasy from her faith in the French system. Indeed both the young people had somewhat changed during these critical years.

As Sophronia began to be surrounded with little Bantams—when she had to face the realities of nature, and her true woman's heart came to find healthy play and outlet in the noblest affections—when she had first a son and heir—then a daughter—then another son—then twins, she began to suspect that humanity could not be wholly regulated by utilitarian philosophy and the Eclectic Religion. These little ones called for some more definite, practical, human, ay! and divine ethics than those of her academy. Every one will say that family cares had weakened her understanding—but no one could have denied that they had softened her heart. We cannot trace the progress of this change. It may partly have contributed to it that, so strongly had the charm of Dr. Dulcis attracted her to him, she had taken pains to cultivate his acquaintance. This brought her into association with Mrs. Dulcis, a woman of rare refinement, of a gentle nature which had been inspired and spiritualised by the daily influence of her husband. The friendship springing from this acquaintance was deep and lasting. Scarcely a week passed without some intercourse between the minister's house at Bellowsbury Square and the aristocratic home in Belgravia. Sophronia often of a Sunday drove to the chapel of the dissenting preacher. In fact she deserted the philosophers in the basest manner, and abjured the French system as a practical absurdity. Exuberant maternity had antidoted theoretic philosophy. Lord Bantam being a man was less affected by the changes and friendships of life; but he entertained for Dr. Dulcis a sincere regard, and viewed his wife's declination with exemplary resignation.

***

II.—The Creed of Party.

THE defeat of the Polkinghorne Government which had taken place a few weeks after our hero's election, led to a dissolution, followed by the formation of a Fogy Ministry. During the intervening month the outbreak of a rebellion in the only rebellious part of the Sovereign's dominions, demanding great and immediate effort and threatening incidentally to involve the country in a war with one of the most powerful of friendly states, had withdrawn the attention of the people from political questions; so that Redistribution was suffered to remain an unsolved problem. Social questions had again come to the front; the more that the pressure of the heavy taxation required for the expenses of military argument with the islanders had roused every one to an appreciation of the value of economy and the necessity of a better organization of Government local and Imperial. Some of the dominions appended to the Empire were exhibiting symptoms of dissatisfaction with the nature of their relations—relations undefined, casual, variable and dependent on the incongruous policy of the Ministers who chanced from time to time to be appointed to the supervision of their affairs. Still the Fogy Cabinet held on its way under the experienced navigation of Mr. Sardonius. It was generally admitted that Mr. Polkinghorne could never form another Minis-

THE CREED OF PARTY.

try, and the leadership of the Popular party was assumed, in virtue of his splendid abilities, by Sir Dudley Wrightman. I need not say that he and the party felt peculiarly and honestly irritated at their prolonged absence from office.

The Session of 18— was opened by a speech from the Throne. It adverted to the happy termination of hostilities in the adjacent island: It spoke of the aspirations of the people for various reforms in Government organization: It set forth a programme of useful measures; *e.g.* for the rigid inspection of various places where dangerous works were carried on: for securing health and cleanliness in great cities: for improving the condition of the agricultural labourer: and for a complete reorganization of the navy. Mr. Sardonius was a minister whose genius was admitted without dissent. Amongst his colleagues, though there were no other geniuses, there were several admirable men of business; and with the generous assistance of his rival, there was no shadow of question that he might during a peaceful Session have passed several measures of immediate and lasting utility.

But the Populars being out of office, like Fogies in the same predicament, as if they were the high-priests of politics, professed to believe that no other legislation could be beneficent than that sanctified by passage through their hands. They loudly exclaimed that the country could not safely entrust to the Fogies the conduct of such important measures; yet they could hardly without stultifying themselves challenge their opponents upon them, since they acknowledged them to be good ones.

Sir Dudley Wrightman and his friends were at their wits' end. He watched the movements of his subtle rival with cat-like vigilance. For many sleepless nights he sat, hat over brow, wearily listening to debates, every now and then rising and launching a Philippic at his smiling antagonist. He challenged him to a division on his foreign policy, but as the foreign minister had done nothing, was beaten. He pursued all the courses habitual to vindictive party jealousy on whatever side of the House. But it was clear that public enthusiasm had not yet been evoked, and the skill of the leader of the Opposition backed by all his satellites had failed to discover any point on which that enthusiasm could be galvanised into action.

Lord Bantam, being in Opposition, worked with his party. He had on several occasions rendered distinguished service by his shrewd, direct, hard-hitting eloquence. On one occasion he brought forward a motion which received some support from the other side, in favour of assistance to British emigrants; and so great was the temptation to the Popular leaders to take advantage of the conjunction, they were nearly committing themselves to a policy that was abhorrent to them. The main constituents of the Popular party were

Prig landholders and employers of labour, to whom State aid in any form was the crudest of absurdities and the direst of chimeras; yet I expect they would have objected to the resolution of society into its original atoms.

It was at this time that Lord Bantam became acquainted with a gentleman who was a member for a Scotch borough. His name was Peregrine. With a very indifferent position in the House he was nevertheless an inveterate busy-body. He had the usual Scotch confidence in himself. It was his conviction that he had repeatedly saved his party, and he earnestly impressed upon its members the virtue of political gratitude. If a vacancy happened in any office when a Popular government was in power, Mr. Peregrine began to frequent the Radical Club, and to show himself in conversation with lounging leaders or Ministers. His invariable disappointment never affected his spirits. He had a faith superior to moving mountains—it was a faith that did not believe in their existence. Taking it into his head that Bantam was making a position in the party, he found an opportunity to accost him in the lobby.

"Lord Bantam," said he, "this seems very hopeless work for us."

"I beg your pardon," said Bantam; "what does?"

"The way the party is going on; no question on which we can challenge Sardonius, and not a ghost of a cry to raise the people."

"Well," said Bantam, "we cannot help that. I am rather inclined to think we ought to rest on our oars awhile. Why should we want to get in? Radicals have nothing to gain by change. The Prigs would like to use our shoulders to stand on until they have won a footing higher up; but it is impossible to construct a pure Radical ministry; and as the Government are passing some harmless and useful measures, why should we interfere with them?"

"Oh!" replied the other, "you must not look at it in that way. What's to become of the party?"

"The party may go to the devil, if it pleases," answered the disloyal young gentleman; "that is of little consequence. Why need we care, if good is being done, and Popular principles are meantime making way? I have no faith in party except as the representative of principle."

Mr. Peregrine stuck his eyeglass into his eye, and examined a new fresco over the arch in the hall where they were standing. It was a great angel clothed in white with a sword in his hand. To his practical Scotch intelligence Bantam's deliverance was puzzling. Said he—

"I don't see the use of party at all, unless it is either in office or fighting for it."

And after this concise statement of the political creed of nine men out of ten in a great legislature, Mr. Peregrine gave up our hero as a moonshiny fop.

III.—Parliamentary Consciences.

Mr. Peregrine's object in addressing himself to Lord Bantam had not been disclosed. The fact was that he had conceived a very clever plan for disconcerting the Fogy Ministry. If there was any question on which a Fogy Ministry was sure to stand firm—on which the most astute of leaders could not hope to dazzle them into metamorphose it was the status of the Church. Now Mr. Peregrine had worked out a combination in his clever brain which he thought strong enough to strike at and overcome that cardinal point of the enemy's works. He took it that the pillar of the Church was the Episcopate. Just at that time a very serious movement against the Episcopate had arisen in the Church itself. Several of the Bishops had assumed an attitude intolerable to many of their clergy and laymen. Discussions had taken place upon the standing and rights of the hierarchy; the papers were filled with details of their enormous salaries; and criticisms on their general assumptions.

"Now," said Mr. Peregrine, "in England and Wales the Church and Dissenters are not quite half and half. In Scotland the very name of a bishop is enough to create a nausea; and everywhere the Roman Catholic bishops and priests are directly interested in the humiliation of the hierarchy of the English Church. Appeal to this combination, sir, for the *Reformation of the Episcopacy*, and you will get up an excitement that must necessarily throw out any government that endeavours to shield it."

Into whose ear do you suppose Mr. Peregrine was pouring this wily incitement? Into those of the Right Honourable Sir Dudley Wrightman, the leader of the Opposition. The only other person present was Mr. Fugleman the Popular Whip, whom Mr. Peregrine had succeeded in talking over, and who had now presented him to his leader.

Sir Dudley received the hint in silence and not without pain. His quick mind at once grasped the ingenuity of the plot, but he was a Churchman—he had a sincere affection for the Church—and to attack it in its most venerable part was to him no grateful task.

A political conscience, especially under party government, is a psychological study. It admits of so much casuistry—of such minute and delicate adjustments to counterbalance fixed principles—of such a number of new patent movements—of such permutations and combinations—and yet all the while the owner of it may be most sincerely accrediting himself the honestest man in Christendom.

IV.—Priest Politics.

WHEN the seed had been sown in the mind of the Popular leader it took some time to germinate. In the first place, as we have seen, the proposition to touch the sacred persons of the Episcopate shocked his sensibilities, ran counter to his earliest and strongest opinions. Again he unconsciously hesitated about the feasibility of the plan. Hence while on the one hand his conscience repelled the temptation held out to it—on the other his mind was weighing the probabilities of success. Let no man throw a stone at him. Human nature, like trout, is apt to take its colour from the bed of the stream in which it swims.

Other members of the party were consulted. Earl Ffowlsmere—a shrewd politician—thought that they might safely embark in the movement; but he pointed out that time was essential, and that the success of the policy might be contingent on the previous success of the party instead of contributing to it: since, in his opinion, it would be necessary as a preliminary move to appoint a few bishops committed to the principle of degrading their own office. It is a pity when the Church becomes the strategy-ground of politicians!

Sir Dudley held many anxious conferences with his followers. He held others with some of the Bishops. He secretly sent for and interrogated the "representatives of the working man;" and lastly he held communication with the Transmontane priesthood. The organs of the party were inspired to blow a soft wooing note to the country.

The Transmontane clergy are ever keenly on the alert

for the rising and falling tides of public opinion. At the very first breath of anti-episcopal feeling, summoned in secret conclave under the astute counsel of their Cardinal head, they had resolved upon their plan of action. If there should turn out to be little life in the agitation, they were to discountenance it, since it was a point of their general policy to flatter the national Church while secretly permeating it as far as possible with their principles and rites. But the Cardinal foresaw that if the impending struggle became serious, the weight of their influence must decide it one way or the other, and he proposed to play for a high reward from whichever side it was to come. One of the most important of important things in the eyes of this clerical party, was the repeal of that law of mortmain, by which they were deprived of not a few death-bed bequests. The harvest of priests is richest on the banks of the Styx; they are not such cheap ferrymen as Charon. They therefore agreed to demand, as the price of their adhesion to either principle, the repeal of the obnoxious law; and since they were appealing to English freemen, and not to Continental bigots and slaves, they agreed to base their assumptions on the extraordinary ground for infallibilists and heretic-burners of CIVIL AND RELIGIOUS LIBERTY! They drew up a pastoral. It was very guarded. It awakened attention without conveying any information. Both political parties scanned it eagerly, but each was puzzled to know which way the wind was blowing.

V.—Transmontane Secrets.

THE private secretary of Mr. Sardonius was a Churchman. He had married a wife a Transmontane, a woman of high culture and great cleverness, with a slight taste for intrigue. The Cardinal's secretary, Father Fugacius, was her intimate friend. It was a curious fact that many of the secrets of Mr. Sardonius found their way to the Cardinal, and that not a few of the Cardinal's views and wishes reached Mr. Sardonius. Thus one day, when the private secretary had received instructions in a number of matters, he inquired of the minister:

"Have you heard of the meeting of Transmontane bishops and their resolutions on the Episcopate question?"

"No," said Sardonius, pricking up his hears. "Where did you hear of it. At the Club? or in the House?"

"Well, the fact is, sir," replied the subordinate, "that Father Fugacius was at my house last evening—he is you know my wife's confessor—and he mentioned it to her, but it was under the seal of the strictest secresy. I hardly know whether——"

"What did he say?" interrupted the Minister peremptorily.

"He said the meeting was decidedly inclined in our favour."

"In favour of the Episcopate?"

"Yes. They seem to have discussed several questions. From what I could gather they were disposed to let the Prison question remain in abeyance; and, as it appears some small sum of £3,000 has been lost to them through the operation of the Mortmain Acts, they intend to appeal to the Government to abolish or modify them."

"Three thousand pounds!" said the acute Minister, with a twinkling eye in his grave face. "Is that what Father Fugacius suggested to your wife as the extent of their losses and the measure of their ambition? Had he said three thousand thousand pounds he would be nearer the mark. But why should they raise that question just now? It would be utterly useless. No Fogy Minister could safely make such a proposal to his party. I should not dare to do it."

The Minister's opinion was scarcely cold ere it reached His Eminence. Before thirty-six hours were gone the latter had also received unsatisfactory reports upon the frame of mind of the other leading members of the Cabinet; and in virtue of a good rule, not to follow a hopeless quest, he turned his attention exclusively to the Popular party. He found them already waiting for him.

***

VI.—A Willing Sacrifice.

His Eminence was closeted with Sir Dudley Wrightman. The Minister had been heard to argue that the Church of England was the purest embodiment of the religion of Christ and the most solid pillar of the State. If his views had undergone any modification, one must admit that to be a characteristic quality of human views in general. The divergence of men from the principles they once held, is the effect of combinations of influences so various, extending over periods so protracted, that it would be impossible for the bitterest cynic to detect the vanishing-point of principle and the initial point of corrupt motive. At this moment Sir Dudley, to tell the truth, would much rather have left the Episcopate alone. But he was in the hands of party—and in the highest circles of statesmanship, party governs with a peremptory rein. It would be impossible to analyse all the reasons which would affect the judgment of men placed on the pinnacle of power, and by their very position challenging the enthusiasm and confidence of a general public.

That day Mr. Fugleman had abundantly satisfied his chief that in the House itself the majority of the Populars were well disposed to the new reform. So many constituencies had pronounced for it that, except in a few cases of more than average independence, a large number of adherents was a matter of necessity. The Extremists being always in favour of change, would he thought go for the movement to a man. A few Prig lords and some county squires were represented to be still unsettled. In any reform of religion the Obstructives are always exceptionally strong, and specially so in the Lords. Mr. Fugleman and others gave it as their opinion that the Transmontanes only could turn the scale.

His Eminence was therefore closeted with the leader of the Opposition——.

VII.—Transmontane Reformers!

At a second meeting of Transmontane ecclesiastics duly summoned, a pastoral was adopted calling upon all their flocks throughout the kingdom to aid the true Church of Christ and the cause of religious Freedom (!) by supporting with their prayers, their votes and their influence, the great movement now pending for the deposition and humiliation of the hierarchy of an Apostate Church.

VIII.—A New Charter.

THERE was high excitement all over the country. The Houses of Parliament and the Clubs began to show signs of political fever. The constituencies were distracted with opposing factions. The Bishops everywhere preached vigorously in their own favour. The dissenting clergy prayed fervently for the degradation of the Bishops. Among the working-men opinions were divided. While a knot of agitating leaders formed a committee to aid the anti-Episcopate movement, large numbers of independent men sagaciously foresaw that this politico-religious agitation in which they were only incidentally interested might delay for many years the settlement of those measures which Mr. Sardonius's government were ready to further. Among the dissentients was Mr. Broadbent, who took up the point so warmly that he urged the Social Anti-Climax League to make it one of their questions and insist on postponing the fate of the Bishops to that of the suffering people.

He came to town to see Lord Bantam.

"My Lord," he said, "I am an old man. I have seen the country struggling through convulsions that among any other people would have been reigns of terror. There is danger about us now. The persistent Prig policy of bamboozling and plastering the people is bearing its fruit in bitter discontent — and now when we might have had something from Mr. Sardonius—we would take a good thing from the devil if he were prime minister—you are all going in for a new political cry."

"Well," said Bantam, "I am entirely with you in all you say—but what is to be done? The Prigs are mad at their long exile from office—the Radicals are piping for some political change—and the country is perhaps getting tired of the monotony of a long-lived ministry."

"Stump the country against this new folly, my Lord. Join the Social Anti-Climax League, and attend its meetings all over the land. We can soon make the Prigs feel our power."

After some hesitation Bantam went so far as to agree to attend a meeting in the district of Bellowsbury, and there in a large hall carefully guarded he was privately introduced to about a hundred members of the League. He then learned for the first time that Broadbent was its Grand President. He was struck with the ability manifested by some of the speakers, especially two or three from the provinces, and was surprised to find how widely the association had extended its roots through the country. This was a meeting of representatives for the purpose of framing a new programme and giving a fresh impetus to the League sentiments. After a discussion of several nights the conference agreed upon the following provisional points of the new charter of English rights :—

1. *All men are equal:*
    Titles are the impertinences of tyranny.
2. *Rights are equal*:
    Power is only legitimate when directed to equalise rights in fact.
3. *The Land is the People's:*
    Its enjoyment must no longer be monopolised.
4. *Work only deserves remuneration:*
    Every worker is entitled of right to a decent house, ground sufficient for his maintenance and a fixed income.
5. *It is the duty of the State to adopt and carry into effect the principles above set forth.*

SUPPLEMENTARY PROPOSITIONS.
6. *Labour is the True Aristocracy:* the supremacy of labour must be acknowledged.
7. *The Capitalist is the tyrant:* he must be blotted out of the social scheme.
8. *Land, Labour, Coöperation, Equalisation—involving the Transfiguration of Labour and the Regeneration of Society:* these are the cardinal heads of the new political gospel—the charter of the liberties of mankind!

When after high debate these propositions had been solemnly affirmed, the League pledged itself to advance them before all other Reforms. Broadbent pressed Lord Bantam to become a member of the society. He at length yielded and committed himself to the principles of the new Charter. In a short time he began to appear at various demonstrations of workpeople in that nursery of agitations the Middle Counties.

⁎

IX.—Death and Sunshine.

IN the midst of these events, there suddenly intervened an incident so strangely out of tune with the loud volcanic heat and motion of our hero's history, that, were we not all familiar with the wonders of life, I should shrink from intruding its seemingly incongruous features into these pages. But life will not adapt itself to the artist's ideal—or is it perhaps that we are not true artists who do not discern beneath the bizarre collations of events a hidden and divine symmetry? Is not he who can most nearly draw the tangled and distracted skeins together into some harmony of design the man who will read life with the truest appreciation and the profoundest artistry?

On his return from a great meeting at Squirmingham, Sophronia informed her husband that Dr. Dulcis lay very ill; that after several days of severe fever he remained so weak as to give his friends grave anxiety. Kelso had gone to his bedside and had tended him with sedulous care. She herself had sometimes relieved the Scotchman for a few hours, and evidently the melancholy intercourse had been productive of a strong effect upon her. Bantam heard the news with unfeigned regret. The quaint, gentle minister had, by his loving tenderness, his illimitable breadth of charity, and the strong earnestness of his religious faith and practice made no slight impression on the young man's heart. When therefore on the succeeding day Kelso came to report that the poor Doctor, though he had recovered his mind, was clearly sinking and had sent to ask Sophronia to visit him, the summons was answered by both Lord and Lady Bantam with very sad alacrity.

The room in which Dr. Dulcis lay dying was a large one with its outlook towards the square, the trees of which had always been a strange pleasure to him as they waved to and fro outside his windows. He had asked them to raise the blind that he might look once more on the gay Spring sky and the familiar branches and the twinkling leaves. Kelso was there and Mrs. Dulcis.

"Those leaves," he was saying, "on their background of glorious blue remind me of man on the panel of eternity. That never passes or alters, though clouds may intervene to shroud it: these die and fall and are blown away—whither?"

"Ah!" said Lord Bantam, as he and Sophronia silently saluted their friends, "Whither, Doctor Dulcis? Who can answer that question?"

"Philosophy cannot, my dear young friend," cried the Doctor. "Positivism declines to do it—Eclecticism strives to ignore the question—and all men lie down before it and wonder."

He paused a few minutes, gazing steadily into the outer light and smiling to himself.

"I am looking out into the heavenly sunlight from the

gloom of this room. This is a true emblem of our souls, prostrate, weak, helpless, hardly able to cry out, darkened in by the curtains of ignorance, folly, and sin—and out there, THERE, the supernal sun-glow, immeasurable and everlasting!"

He turned to Lord and Lady Bantam.

"My friends," said he, "it is well that you, in the zenith of life and prosperity and intellectual activities, should look upon this scene. Here am I stretched upon the rack of the inevitable. There is no Eclectic formula for our conduct in the Valley of the Shadow of Death, except obliviousness and resignation. For me there is more—there is life and hope and peace. Christ is here with help and promise. Christ goes before and clears a shining way. I needed just now a friendly hand to draw yon curtain, and let in the fulness of the sunlight. So we all need the loving hand of Christ to unveil for us the curtained abysm of God's shining infinity—Christ only!" These words he repeated several times, "Christ only."

Bantam, respecting the dying man's enthusiasm, replied with a whisper of sympathy.

Doctor Dulcis looked round for his children, the haze was dimming his eyes. They were called in. The fair-crowned child of former days was now a fine young woman, and the velvet-coated boy had developed into a jacketed stripling, with student paleness and melancholy eyes. As they all drew near his bedside, he gave them one by one his blessing, and charged them to meet him in heaven, with a confidence as great as he would have shown in engaging them to meet him at the house of a friend.

"Now," said he, "sing our Sabbath hymn. Virginia, I cannot blow the bellows for you now, but you need no music! I think I hear another organ playing, but it sounds far away. 'The sands of time are sinking—'"

As he folded his hands on his bosom, and lay back on his pillow, his children set up softly, to a plaintive air, the familiar hymn he had asked for :—

> The sands of Time are sinking,
>   The dawn of heaven breaks;
> The summer morn I've sighed for,
>   The fair sweet morn awakes.
> Dark, dark hath been the midnight,
>   But dayspring is at hand,
> And glory, glory dwelleth
>   In Immanuel's land.
>
> Oh! Christ he is the fountain,
>   The deep sweet well of love;
> The streams of earth I've tasted—
>   More deep I'll drink above.
> There to an ocean fulness
>   His mercy doth expand,
> And glory, glory dwelleth
>   In Immanuel's land.
>
> With mercy and with judgment,
>   My web of time he wove,
> And aye the dews of sorrow
>   Were lustered by His love.

> I'll bless the hand that guided,
> I'll bless the heart that planned,
> When throned where glory dwelleth,
> In Immanuel's land!

—Just then a brighter smile transfigured his pale features as sudden sunlight glints over a corn-field. Mrs. Dulcis clasped her hands and hung over him, looking eagerly down into the face that was upturned towards her and Heaven! .... It was now but a Parian mask with a stony smile. Doctor Dulcis was no longer there.

Not a word was said. The widowed woman was weeping in Sophronia's arms. Kelso had buried his face in the pillow near which he had been leaning, and his hard northern frame shook with emotion. The choristers divining the awful mystery, broke into sobs subdued by their fear. Bantam restrained himself only by a powerful effort, and finally rushed from the room.

The Eclectic Religion has its practical beauties, its brilliant æsthetic attractions, its noble sentiments and principles, its healthy incredulities, but the young Lord questioned in his soul that hour if it could ever make men face death as they would look upon sunshine and roses.

* *
*

X.—Party *versus* Principles.

Lord Bantam's provincial exercitations began to create a prodigious feeling in the country. There never had been, the Prigs avowed, an instance of a man so unconscientiously faithless to party. Candid men might have said that it was rare now-a-days to find a man so unselfishly faithful to principle. Mr. Fugleman, at the request of the Premier, went to Lord Ffowlsmere and told him what he knew better than Mr. Fugleman, that his son was spoiling the game and must be silenced. The Earl, sending for the political prodigal, and rating him most sternly, threatened him with his lasting resentment, if he did not keep quiet.

"You cannot desert your party at such a time!" cried the Earl. "It is unprecedented. It is indecent! No one, not even the most priggish young peacocks of politics or the most discontented place-hunters would think of setting their own opinions against those of their leaders in a crisis!"

"I am always deeply sorrowful to be obliged to disagree with you, my dear father; but I see so clearly the nature of this agitation; its utter hollowness and want of principle: that nothing shall induce me, if you are determined to go on, to vote for the motion. This movement has been invented and fanned into life simply for one purpose, to place our party in power. I do the leaders, among them yourself, the justice to believe that you honestly consider this to be a paramount duty and the only hope of progress. But why should you evoke religious and political animosities at a time when a programme of social reform still lies unattempted before the country? Is it of greater importance that the lives of a hundred thousand persons a year, more or less, should be lost from neglect of sanitary legislation, the regulation of mines, or the better inspection of factories, than that an ecclesiastical system should be made more symmetrically perfect or more consonant with theoretical freedom by deposing a score of bishops?"

Granted the young lord was perverse, egotistic and not amenable to discipline, it must be admitted that there was some reason in his madness.

XI.—A Constitutional Crisis.

THE time was now deemed ripe by the Popular leaders to strike their blow, and Sir Dudley Wrightman gave notice of his intention to move that, "In the opinion of this House, the present status and emoluments of the Bishops of the Church of England were inconsistent with civil and religious liberty and the good of these realms; and that an humble address be presented to Her Majesty praying her to appoint a Commission to enquire into the present condition of the office of the Episcopate of the Church of England, and to take account of the endowments thereof, and to report upon the best means of reforming the said office."

Every nerve was strained on either side. When Sir

A CONSTITUTIONAL CRISIS.   247

Dudley Wrightman presented petitions from half the fellows of the Universities in favour of the proposed reform, Mr. Sardonius brought into the House a vast memorial from a million of Obstructive working men who declared the Episcopate to be the lodestar of their liberties. When a red-hot Obstructive procured the signatures of three hundred Wesleyan ministers in favour of Bishoprics, an impertinent Radical came forward with a counter-petition from eighteen of the leading philosophers of the day. The Whips and their aides-de-camp on both sides were engaged in eager canvassing, and—I am bound to tell—in making arrangements that would never have passed the keen criticisms of an Election Judge, had they been the acts of simple attorneys or agents in a local contest. Peremptory letters and telegrams brought home every available member from America, from Egypt, from Algiers; dying men from Mentone: hypochondriac legislators from the various "waters": parliamentary sportsmen from Sweden: an Admiralty steam-yacht was put into requisition to hunt up a cruising party of Fogies: and the Populars arranged for the carriage to the division of a Parliamentary patient afflicted with small-pox, who was to be dressed in clothes steeped in the latest disinfectant. It is thus that in England preparations are made for the decision of great constitutional issues involving the profoundest principles of government.

One need not describe at length the debate on the

motion. How on the critical evening the lobbies were thronged with members and with eager hunters after the qualified treat of a sitting in the gallery. How the police and doorkeepers made a rich harvest of sovereigns from persons unprovided with tickets, while those who had thoughtfully procured their orders a week beforehand cooled themselves in a row on a stone seat in St. Stephen's Hall or heated themselves in altercations with the equally stony guardians of the portal. Sir Dudley Wrightman made a magnificent speech. It was three hours long. It traced the history of Episcopacy from the time of Peter and Judas; it reviewed the long line of the English hierarchy; it gave statistics of the value of each bishopric and compared them with the number of souls cured by each bishop; it criticised the assumption of the present tenants; it pointed out how inconsistent those were with the modern ideas of liberty; it compared the incubus of the Episcopacy upon the Church to the Old Man of the Mountain, and hinted that the legs were none the less bearable from the fact of their being enveloped in silk stockings and gaiters; it showed the injustice done to the Transmontane hierarchy by the inequality of their status; and finally it concluded with a grand peroration in which he averred that the Church no longer fanned to perilous somnolency by the silken wings of the black vampires which drew her lifeblood while they pleased her sense, would wake to new and glorious energies of being, &c. &c.

As soon as the motion had been seconded by Mr. Kitchingman, a rising politician, our **hero** rose and amidst ringing and reiterated cheers from the Fogy benches declared himself in favour of the principles enunciated by his leader—but opposed to the motion. He denounced it as an ill-advised, ill-timed and dangerous trifling with the interests of the body politic: he warned the House that in view of the uneasy symptoms exhibited by the working classes safety demanded immediate attention to far different legislation.

"**Let** me try to show the House," said Bantam shrewdly, " whereon the artisan discontent builds itself, and why it is taking the shape of bold revolutionary demand instead of calm constitutional procedure. Consider all the measures introduced into Parliament during the past ten years. **How** many there have been of a distinctively political character! How many have dealt thoughtfully with the interests of the higher and middle classes! And how many acts of beneficent legislation have been modified, crippled or postponed altogether in the same selfish interests! Education—the education for these very classes, was last year granted to them it is true, but granted to them upon terms they do not approve—granted to them subject to modifications introduced in the interests of Fogyism and bigotry. Had this House been constituted with a due share of artisan representation, is it possible that that scheme could ever have received the assent of Parliament; would a Fogy

Government ever have been permitted to conduct the legislation on that question? Again, we, a select body of aristocrats, manufacturers and stock-jobbers, undertook to legislate for the associations formed by working men for self-preservation and to uphold the rights of labour. By you these are treated as tyrannical instruments of compulsion; but you forget that the inordinate and natural advantages of capital in this country enabled it to hold labour in iron bonds, and to press it down with hydraulic force; and that if now the balance is at all better adjusted, the improvement is due to these associations. Yet when you are appealed to for a generous concession to them of such rights and privileges as are accorded to any ordinary commercial association, you testify your fear of what you are obliged to concede with one hand, by threatening with the other! Again, take another case, you proclaim the dogma of Government non-intervention in many hopeful utilitarian projects, but some years since a professedly Popular government turned round upon friendly associations framed for mutual help, and abnegating the doctrine of their clique that men should take care of themselves, most inconsistently organized an inquisitorial machinery to protect, as they pretended, the artisans from cheating each other. Where you *can* do anything, you fail; when you see your way to interfere in anything with a hope of acquiring greater power, you are too quick for action. From year to year you suffer thousands of lives to remain subjected to terrible, hourly danger,— a danger every now and then culminating in some awful catastrophe, too often the result of the diabolical selfishness, niggardliness, and indifference of men rolling in money, who regard more the interests of their cattle than the well-being and safety of those whose labours win their wealth. So, in a hundred ways, you defeat, you disconcert, you grind down, you obstruct, you madden the surging masses, and no wonder they feel themselves to be driven to but one remedy—the remedy of Continental reformers—revolution. Revolution is not necessary. I believe that ample capacities of good still live in our time-honoured constitution; but, Sir, for God's sake, I call upon every lover of his country, and every lover of himself, to make this House more flexible; make its policy less rigid : bring it into readier sympathy with the great millions outside—or look out for your property and your lives!"

One sees that there was a good deal of fluent Kelsoism in this speech. The House heard it with curiosity. The Fogies during the debate made a good deal out of it, but, though not a few Populars in their secret consciences went with the too impulsive orator, the claims of party and their own interest tied them down to their predetermined votes. On the third night of the debate, after a terribly sarcastic speech from Mr. Sardonius and a fine reply from his rival, the ministry were defeated by the small majority of *nine* and resolved to appeal to the country.

Meanwhile colliery explosions continued to blow their scores at a time of human machines into cinders, leaving ample families to test the charity of the ratepayers: big brewers or distillers, and little publicans continued to fatten on the blown corpses of the prey they pursued with unrestricted licence: men and women perished in filth and effluvia carefully maintained for the purpose of assisting their exit from a world of rates and taxes by thoughtful "guardians of the poor:" an epidemic, sweeping over the Continent, waved its black flag across the Channel towards the hopeful fields where no legislation and the principles of Magna Charta combined to invite its attack: and the navy, the guardian of the honour and existence of free England, was left to be reformed in the face of the enemy.

It is thus that party government, amidst its rivalries and throes, jerks aside to chance, or delay, or oblivion, the precious interests of millions; and discounts, at increasing usury, the dwindling chances of social conservation.

The country being agitated by the contested election, the leaders of the Social Anti-Climax League proposed to take advantage of the excitement to advance its principles. A demonstration in the metropolis of half-a-million of men was projected; through the provinces local meetings were to be held; and where favourable opportunities arose, attempts were to be made by manifestations of force to intimidate constituencies into the adoption of proletarian candidates. For this purpose an extensive organization in military fashion was successfully instituted with the aid of some Poles and other Continentals, to whom such business was only too familiar. Secret depôts of arms were established; but, with the usual blindness of revolutionaries, the illegality of elections won under such circumstances never seems to have struck them. I need not say that the young Lord was not informed of these grave intentions and preparations: he was energetically pursuing the theoretic Commune—his coadjutors, too practical to be dazzled by that phantom, were aiming at the disintegration of society.

PART VIII.

HOW HE CAME TO HIS ESTATE.

I.—The Ruling Passion Strong in Death.

WHILE the great proletarian movement was pending, and Lord Bantam at Shufflestraw Castle was concerting with Broadbent measures that would have led to the conversion of that feudal domain into a middle age community, the noble agitator was suddenly summoned to London by the information that the Earl had had a seizure and was lying in a precarious state at the town mansion. The young Lord's feelings as he pursued his rapid journey to the metropolis were naturally strange and tumultuous. It seemed as if all he had been doing had been done without reference to the contingency now irresistibly suggested to his mind. So often do we act with one eye blinded to the possibilities of our existence!

When he reached the house in Hiton Place, the aspect of old Trayfoot was far from reassuring.

"The Earl is very ill, my Lawd: there are two doctors with him now. He recovered consciousness about an hour since, but his weakness gives great alarm. The Countess is with him, my Lawd."

Entering the ante-room, the young Lord signed to one of the physicians, who coming out, gave his hand a peculiar pressure as he spoke to him.

"You must go in at once, my Lord. He has asked for you two or three times."

The Earl noticing the doctor's movement with the quick susceptibility of illness, said:

"Is Albert come?"

Lord Bantam went forward. His mother holding the Earl's hand looked at her husband with the firmness of a true woman but with a pallid face. Her white hair and clear-cut features seemed to shine with a sort of silver light in the shadowy room.

As Lord Bantam took his other hand, the Earl's features lighted up, and for a moment or two wore the aspect so familiar to frequenters of the House of Peers when he was about to address them in a great debate.

"Albert," he said, "you will soon be Lord Ffowlsmere——" The Countess could not restrain the hand that softly stayed his lips; but the Earl went on. "Yes, I know it is coming—it has come at last. You have latterly given me some anxiety. I deeply and sincerely regretted the wildness of your opinions, because I knew the time would arrive when you *must give them up*. I knew it was coming—it was coming——"

Lord Bantam remained silent, and watched with a fascinated gaze the weak breathings of the old Earl as he paused for a few moments.

"First," he said, " I wish to advise you to be careful of your estate. By judicious management and constant watchfulness, I have added to it nearly two millions sterling. Don't trust any one but yourself, and beware of attorneys. I always said, the devil exhausted his ingenuity in deceiving Eve and it was left to mankind to invent an attorney. Be your own lawyer and you will have few lawsuits."—

He paused again.

"As to your politics," he continued, "you have gone too far. I never objected to your thinking for yourself. A young man is none the worse for being original and active; but there is no excuse for being revolutionary. I wished to see and warn you before I died. You are about to succeed," he went on with a firm proud voice, "to the richest title in England—be worthy of it. A peer cannot be a proletarian. You would be judicious to acquiesce in the progressive tendencies of the day; but with the interests we have at stake, we cannot afford to do more than acquiesce. You will learn that it is your interest to follow the people not to prompt them. Believe me, on my dying bed I solemnly tell you, the policy of my life has been a Prig policy—and the Prig policy is the middle course which is the safety of the aristocracy of this kingdom. I had hoped to see you take the lead in that policy.—Yes!" said the Earl with sudden vehemence and raising his voice. "I say, my Lords, that I am prepared to defend to the death, that policy by which the ancient institutions of this nation are upheld in their integrity while reform pursues its course with secure, temperate, and gradual footsteps! I say――."

The strained voice dropped, and in a moment the Countess's arm was under the white head, and it lay with closed eyes upon her shoulder. . . . . . For an instant the lips moved. It was only a whisper—

> "In Holland there dwelt a Mynheer Von Clam,—
> And every morning he said――"

—but Earl Ffowlsmere never said "I am" again.

II.—In the Grain.

THE new Earl, clad in a simple suit of black, was sitting in that study into which Trayfoot more than twenty-six years before, had precipitately borne the announcement of his birth to the man now lying dead in the chamber above.

Trayfoot, grey and portly, clad in the blackest black, was also there. The young Peer was surrounded by papers. In his hand he held a well-covered sheet of foolscap.

"This estimate of Rooking's, Trayfoot, is very excessive. I hope," said he, looking hard at the old man,

S

"you have not arranged to take a commission on my father's funeral?"

"Certainly not, your Lawdship," said Trayfoot, rather indignantly. "Those people never pay commissions."

"Then," said the Earl, "this bill is extortionate. It makes the honour of a burial in Westminster Abbey altogether too dear.. Seven hundred and seventy pounds! Twenty-five guineas for the hearse: ten guineas for the use of a 'velvet pall satin lined :' 'two hundred and ten silk hatbands,' at thirty shillings each! What do you think of it?"

"It's extortionate, as your Lawdship says; but they never alter their estimates, I'm told."

Trayfoot had in fact demanded of the undertakers one per cent. on their bill, which they had curtly refused. His concurrence with the young Earl's opinion was therefore genuine.

"Well now," said our hero, sighing, "I desire every respect to be paid to my honoured father's memory, and nearly the whole of the ministry will be at this funeral, therefore I suppose we must accept this estimate."

"They said, my Lawd, that an estimate for a funeral in Westminster Abbey was very unusual, and that they only gave it in consideration of your Lawdship's high position, but they would not be bound by it within a few hundred pounds or so."

Trayfoot was having his revenge.

"Oh! they said that did they? But this estimate I

see is signed by them—and I shall hold them strictly to it. They have clearly put down double the number of hatbands that will be required. I wish you therefore on the day of the funeral to keep a strict watch and take a memorandum of the number actually supplied. You will also be good enough to count the number of attendants and servitors. My father must be buried without regard to expense, but I will not be imposed upon."

III.—Philosophy and Fact.

The funeral over and Messrs. Rookings' bill triumphantly reduced by a clearly proved overcharge of £167, which made them regret their parsimony to Trayfoot, the Earl and Countess with their children left London for Shufflestraw Castle. There for a week the young Peer gave himself up to a mastery of the whole of the estate accounts. It was some satisfaction to find that his father's unrivalled business powers had left him nothing to criticise.

Scarcely a week had passed when he was one day surprised by an intimation from his servants that a large body of rough-looking men headed by Broadbent, had passed the East Lodge and was approaching the Castle. The Earl immediately sent off a mounted groom to the

Ffowlsmere Police Station, asking that a detachment of the force might be sent to his assistance. All the males employed in the Castle or surrounding grounds were collected and hastily armed. They were however disposed out of sight. As the proletarians, marching three abreast turned the last curve of the avenue towards the great gate of the Castle, the Earl, accompanied by Trayfoot, the bailiff and a stalwart servitor, descended to the steps which led from the drawbridge and awaited the arrival of his unwelcome visitors. His appearance was greeted by a ringing cheer which spite of himself agitated him greatly. Drawing them up opposite the steps, their leader, remaining covered, approached Lord Ffowlsmere and familiarly offered him his hand, which the other took with silent and cold placidity.

"I sympathise deeply with your loss, my brother citizen," said the old man. "Humanity is the same everywhere, and rank foregoes no sorrow. But the past is past. Let the dead bury their dead. Life is in the present and before us. We now have to deal with the fact of your auspicious succession to the dignities and possessions of your father. On this we have come to congratulate you and ourselves and the people of England."

A blush passed over the Earl's face as he silently bowed an acknowledgment.

"We have communicated with our friends all over the country, and have drawn up an address, which this deputation is here to present to you on behalf of the Social Anti-Climax League."

Once more the Earl saw Broadbent draw forth those broad-rimmed spectacles and unfold a sheet of proletarian paper. Once more did the old man's gruff voice read to him with uncouth emphasis a proletarian address. It was——

> "*From the Presidents, Vice-presidents, Council and Associates of the Social Anti-Climax League of the People of England to their fellow-citizen and brother-member, Albert Alfred Augustus Adolphus Loftus Cicely Chester Bantam, commonly called Lord Bantam, and now termed Earl of Ffowlsmere.*"

It stated that as brethren of one "whom we hold in high regard, we heartily express our sympathies with you in the severe and sudden affliction which has befallen you; and we trust that you will be sustained in it by that pure and high philosophy, which recognising in every event the movement of the inevitable, rests in the supreme dignity of resignation."

It proceeded to congratulate him on the attainment of a position which would enable him to carry out practically the principles he had so nobly professed; it referred to the propositions of the Bellowsbury Charter; it reminded him that he had declared his adhesion to them;

it expressed the hopes kindled in their bosoms by his succession to his enormous wealth; and concluded thus:

> *"We, therefore, your brother citizens and associates in the League, relying on your honesty and sincerity, invite and pray you to place yourself at the head of the new, great social movement for the transfiguration of Labour and the regeneration of Society."*

The Earl received the address with visible embarrassment. Immediately facing him was the sturdy trunk and leonine head of the old shoemaker, and below were drawn up his late associates in the Social Anti-Climax League, all waiting for him to take the lead in the transfiguration of Labour. How different is theoretic Radicalism from Communistic practice! He hesitated.

"Well, my Lord," said Broadbent, "we await your answer. Surely you have made up your mind. We are prepared to follow you to the death."

"No doubt—a—Mr.—Broadbent; but, Mr. Broadbent and my good friends, I—I—have lately had to reconsider with some care the subject of your address, and—in fact, gentlemen—I have changed my mind."

FINIS.

www.ingramcontent.com/pod-product-compliance
Lightning Source LLC
Chambersburg PA
CBHW032008230426
43672CB00010B/2287